The Poet and the Professor

Level 2

Poems for Building Reading Skills

Authors

Timothy Rasinski, Ph.D., and Karen McGuigan Brothers

Contributing Author

Jodene Lynn Smith, M.A.

SHELL EDUCATION

Publishing Credits

Dona Herweck Rice, *Editor-in-Chief*; Lee Aucoin, *Creative Director*; Don Tran, *Print Production Manager;* Timothy J. Bradley, *Illustration Manager*; Conni Medina, M.S.Ed., *Editorial Director*; Evelyn Garcia, *Associate Editor*; Robin Erickson, *Interior Layout Designer;* Ana Clark, Heidi Schmidt, *Illustrators*; Corinne Burton, M.S.Ed., *Publisher*

McREL Standards © 2004 www.mcrel.org/standards-benchmarks

All recordings performed by Holly Eiholzer. Recorded, edited, and mastered by Scott Zschomler at Lunar Studios.

Shell Education
5301 Oceanus Drive
Huntington Beach, CA 92649-1030
http://www.shelleducation.com

ISBN 978-1-4258-0676-7

Printed in USA BRP001

Table of Contents

Developing students' reading skills is a critical skill that begins in the primary grades. As you use the poems, lessons, and activities in this book, you will not only be providing instruction based on solid educational research, but also giving students opportunities to learn and practice specific academic standards.

The Poet and the Professor: Poems for Building Reading Skills is designed to provide high-interest instructional texts and lessons based on best practices in reading education. Each poem has an accompanying lesson plan with ideas for phonemic awareness, phonics, vocabulary, fluency, and comprehension activities based on the poem.

In an effort to identify the best practices in reading instruction, the National Reading Panel (2000) reviewed thousands of studies to determine key elements of effective reading instruction. The five essential areas of reading instruction are: phonemic awareness, phonics, vocabulary, fluency, and comprehension. The lessons in this book reflect these five elements of reading instruction.

Phonemic Awareness

Phonemic awareness refers to the awareness of the sounds of language and how language sounds work together to create words. Research shows that phonemic awareness is an excellent predictor of a student's future reading success (Adams 1990; Stanovich 1986; Yopp 1988). Although many students develop phonemic awareness informally, evidence suggests that phonemic awareness can be developed through direct instruction (Ball and Blachman 1991). Activities such as identifying, isolating, and categorizing phonemes, blending sounds to make words, segmenting sounds in words, and adding, deleting, and substituting phonemes require students to manipulate sounds in order to gain a better understanding of words (Yopp 1992; National Reading Panel 2000).

Each lesson in *The Poet and the Professor: Poems for Building Reading Skills* provides a phonemic awareness activity to train students in this important reading skill. Using words from the poem as a springboard, students are asked to manipulate phonemes. Although most of the phonemic awareness tasks are presented orally, there are also numerous activity pages that support phonemic awareness concepts. (See the Activity Skill—Correlation Chart on page 14.)

Phonics

During phonics instruction, students connect language sounds with corresponding written letters to see how they work together to form words that can be both read and written. Based on its review of studies, the National Reading Panel reports that explicit and systematic phonics instruction is an effective way to help students gain and apply knowledge of letter/sound relationships. The poems and activities in this book provide explicit ways to teach and reinforce phonics concepts appropriate to the primary grades.

The activities and teaching suggestions provided in each lesson are designed to help students improve word recognition and spelling skills. The activities focus on words or spelling patterns found in the poems.

Vocabulary

Our vocabulary consists of the words we know and use. These words help us communicate both verbally and in writing and also assist in reading comprehension. Vocabulary instruction can have direct effects on reading comprehension (Pressley 2002). Students who understand the words they read are more likely to comprehend the texts they read.

Students expand their vocabularies in many different ways. During direct word instruction, definitions are provided, as well as modeling and practice for using specific words in meaningful ways. Providing students with as few as two direct instructional strategies, allows them to understand the word when encountering it within a text (Baker, Simmons, and Kameenui 1998). The goal is to make students comfortable using new words in their own oral and written vocabularies through multiple, meaningful encounters with those words.

The vocabulary section of each lesson provides strategies and ideas for direct, meaningful instruction of words used in the poems. Words or phrases that may be unfamiliar or challenging to students have been selected from the poems for instruction. Students may be more familiar with some words than others. The purpose of this section is to provide in-depth instruction for words in the poems, thereby teaching meanings of new words and deepening understanding of those the student knows.

Fluency

Fluency refers to a student's ability to read accurately, effortlessly, and with expression (Rasinski 2003). Fluency instruction is important because fluent readers are better able to focus their attention on comprehension. Readers have a limited amount of attention to expend for reading. Students who use too much attention on word decoding understand less of what they read because they do not sufficiently focus attention on gaining meaning from the text (LaBerge and Samuels 1974).

One method of helping students gain fluency is repeated readings of a text. Studies on repeated readings have shown many benefits for readers. Students increase their comprehension as they group words in text into meaningful segments marked by expressive reading (O'Shea and Sindelar 1983). This method also helps students remember important information from a passage, including vocabulary (Bromage and Mayer 1986). Fluency rates and accurate word recognition can increase as students read other passages of equal or greater difficulty after mastering the original passage (Samuels 1979).

Providing meaningful and fun ways for students to return to a text can be a challenge. Poems are ideal texts for reading, rereading, and performing. The fluency section of each lesson and the corresponding activity pages give suggestions for students to reread the poems in fun, meaningful, and authentic ways that will provide the benefits that research shows for repeated readings.

Comprehension

We read for many different reasons—to learn something new, to enjoy a story, and to experience language are a few examples. Effective reading instruction must include teaching strategies that students can use to increase comprehension. Expert readers freely and appropriately use a variety of strategies to gain understanding as they read. Students need to effectively monitor their reading to maintain understanding and realize when their understanding has collapsed (Hosenfeld 1993). There are many effective strategies that teachers can use with students to assist with reading comprehension. These include using graphic organizers (Jensen 1998), predicting, rephrasing, answering questions, and generating questions (Bottomley and Osborn 1993). Teaching and modeling reading comprehension strategies through structured and explicit instruction enables students to learn how to comprehend text (Rosenshine and Meister 1994). The result of both explicit teaching and modeling is that students learn when and how to use these strategies to construct meaning (Carter 1997).

The comprehension section of each lesson provides strategies to help students increase their understanding of the poems. The suggestions vary from lesson to lesson, but include questions to ask students, discussion ideas, ways for students to demonstrate their understanding of the poem, and ideas for helping students make text-to-self and text-to-life connections. Many of the ideas and strategies can be used with any of the poems. Consider adapting your favorite comprehension ideas or strategies to other poems.

Word Study Extension

In a survey of words, Edward Fry (1998) found that by adding a consonant to the beginning of 38 rimes (the vowel plus the remaining consonants in a word, e.g., *ed, it, op*), more than 600 words can be read. This is a staggering and powerful number of words for a beginning reader to know. By studying and analyzing spelling patterns, students practice consolidating larger units of words or letter patterns that can then be applied to reading other words (Gaskins et al. 1997). Gaskins states, "Knowing consolidated units makes it easier to read and remember multisyllabic words as sight words, for it enables readers to deal with chunks of letters rather than each individual letter." The goal of teaching students to work with spelling patterns is to provide them with strategies for decoding words rapidly to increase fluency and comprehension.

A Word Study page is provided for each poem. First, students identify and categorize words from the poem and then build on that knowledge to create and categorize new words based on targeted rimes. For the second activity, students contextualize words by completing cloze sentences.

Using the poems, lessons, and activity pages in *The Poet and the Professor: Poems for Building Reading Skills* will provide a research-based and engaging way to teach elements essential to any reading program. By studying the poems in this book, students will practice and gain important strategies that will develop and strengthen their reading skills. Happy poetry reading!

Differentiation

Classrooms have evolved into diverse pools of learners including gifted students, English language learners, high achievers, learning-disabled students, underachievers, and average achievers. Teachers are expected to meet these diverse needs in one classroom. Differentiation encompasses what is taught, how it is taught, and the products students create to show what they have learned. These categories are often referred to as content, process, and product:

- Differentiating by content means putting more depth into the curriculum by organizing the curriculum concepts and structure of knowledge.
- Differentiating by process requires the use of varied instructional techniques and materials to enhance learning.
- Differentiating by product means that children are asked to show their learning in ways that will enhance their cognitive development and personal expression.

Teachers can keep these categories in mind as they plan instruction that will best meet the needs of their students.

Differentiating for Below-Grade-Level Students

Below-grade-level students will need concepts made more concrete for them. They may also need extra guidance in developing oral and written language. By receiving extra support and understanding, these students will feel more secure and have greater success. Suggested ideas include:

- Allow partner work for instructional activities.
- Allocate extra practice time.
- Allow for kinesthetic (hands-on) activities where appropriate.

Differentiating for Above-Grade-Level Students

These students usually learn concepts very quickly. The activities and end products can be adapted to be appropriate for individual students. Suggested ideas include:

- Assign students the activities that represent more complex concepts.
- Assign more complex oral and written responses.
- Have students design their own learning strategies and share them with the class.

Differentiating for English Language Learners

English language learners are an ever-increasing percentage of our school-age population. Like all students, English language learners need teachers who have a strong knowledge base and commitment to developing students' language. It is crucial that teachers work carefully to develop English language learners' academic vocabularies. Teachers should incorporate the following important practices:

- Create a comfortable atmosphere that encourages students to use language.
- Respect and draw on students' backgrounds and experiences and build connections between the known and the new.
- Model and scaffold language use.
- Make use of realia, concrete materials, visuals, pantomime, and other nonlinguistic representations of concepts to make input comprehensible. Write new words on the board as they are shared or provide each student with a set of cards that contain the words.
- Provide wait time to allow students the opportunity to gather their thoughts.

Differentiating by Proficiency Levels for English Language Learners

All teachers should know the levels of language acquisition for each of their English language learners. Knowing these levels will help to plan instruction. (The category titles vary from district to district or state to state, but the general descriptions are common.) Students at level 1 will need a lot of language support in all the activities. Using visuals to support oral and written language will help to make the language more comprehensible. These students "often understand much more than they are able to express" (Herrell and Jordan 2004). It is the teacher's job to move them from listening to language to expressing language. Students at levels 2 and 3 will benefit from pair work in speaking tasks, but they will need additional individual support during writing and reading tasks. Students at levels 4 and 5 (or 6, in some cases) may appear to be fully proficient in the English language. However, because they are English language learners, they may still struggle with comprehending the academic language used during instruction. They may also struggle with reading and writing.

The following chart shows the proficiency levels at a quick glance. The levels are based on the World-Class Instructional Design and Assessment (WIDA) Consortium (WIDA 2007).

Proficiency Levels at a Quick Glance

<table>
<tr><th>Proficiency Level</th><th>Questions to Ask</th><th colspan="3">Activities/Actions</th></tr>
<tr><td rowspan="2">Level 1—Entering
minimal comprehension
no verbal production</td><td rowspan="2">Where is…?
What examples do you see?
What are the parts of…?</td><td>listen</td><td>draw</td><td>mime</td></tr>
<tr><td>point</td><td>circle</td><td>respond (one or two words)</td></tr>
<tr><td rowspan="2">Level 2—Beginning
limited comprehension
short spoken phrases</td><td rowspan="2">Can you list three…?
What facts or ideas show…?
What do the facts mean?</td><td>move</td><td>select</td><td>act/act out</td></tr>
<tr><td>match</td><td>choose</td><td>list</td></tr>
<tr><td rowspan="2">Level 3—Developing
increased comprehension
simple sentences</td><td rowspan="2">How did ____ happen?
Why do you think…?
If you could __, what would you do?</td><td>name</td><td>list</td><td>respond (phrases or sentences)</td></tr>
<tr><td>label</td><td>categorize</td><td>tell/say</td></tr>
<tr><td rowspan="3">Level 4—Expanding
very good comprehension
some errors in speech</td><td rowspan="3">How would you show…?
What would result if…?
Why is this important?</td><td>recall</td><td>retell</td><td>define</td></tr>
<tr><td>compare/ contrast</td><td>explain</td><td>summarize</td></tr>
<tr><td>describe</td><td>role-play</td><td>restate</td></tr>
<tr><td rowspan="3">Level 5—Bridging
comprehension comparable to native-English speakers
speaks using complex sentences</td><td rowspan="3">What is meant by…?
What is an original way to show…?
Why is it better that…?</td><td>analyze</td><td>defend</td><td>complete</td></tr>
<tr><td>evaluate</td><td>justify</td><td>support</td></tr>
<tr><td>create</td><td>describe</td><td>express</td></tr>
</table>

How to Use This Book

The Poet and the Professor: Poems for Building Reading Skills is a succession of lessons built around a compilation of poems. The program includes this book (which is a teacher's resource for using the poems to build reading skills), and the Digital Resources.

This book features 30 original poems. Accompanying each poem is a lesson plan that contains the sections Phonemic Awareness, Phonics, Vocabulary, Fluency, Comprehension, and Word Study Extension. Information and ideas about how to relate the poem to each of these areas is provided on this page. For more information about each section, see the Research section of this book (pp. 4–6). In addition, two activity pages are provided that correspond to selected sections of the lesson plan.

The Digital Resources contain recordings of each of the poems in the book. Students can follow the text on their own copies of the poem pages, on an interactive whiteboard, or on an overhead projector.

The Digital Resources contain a variety of resources that can be used to enhance the lessons provided in this book. The poem pages can be photocopied on a transparency, displayed on an interactive whiteboard, or printed and copied for each student. The activity pages are included in the Digital Resources.

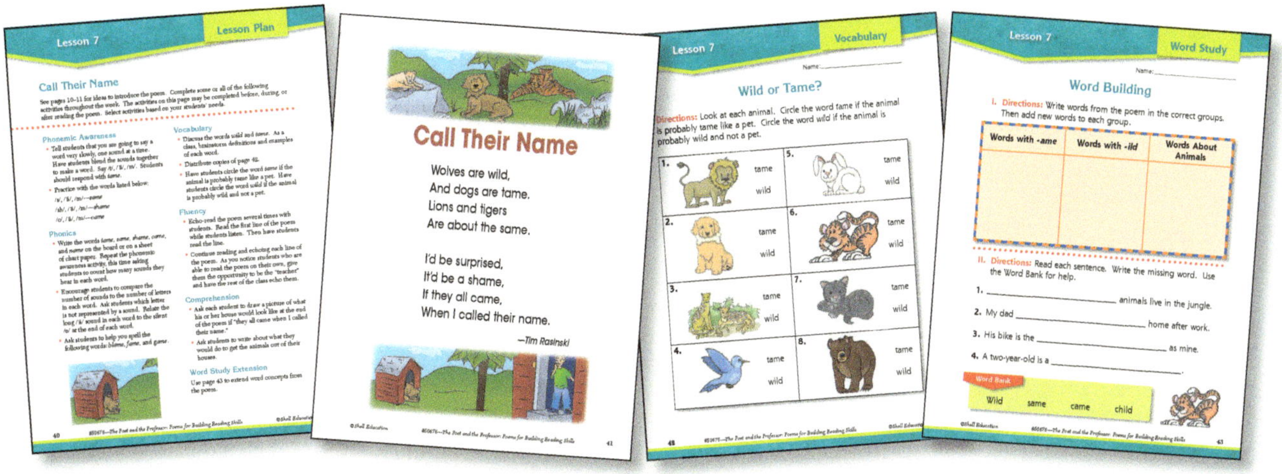

The Poet and the Professor: Poems for Building Reading Skills has been designed to supplement any reading language arts program. The following is a suggested routine for incorporating the poetry, reading comprehension, standards based skills, and word study activities into your weekly lessons.

Day	Suggested Instructional Plan
Day 1	• Display the poem. Provide a copy of the poem to each student. Read the poem with an expressive voice. Point to the words as you read the poem. • Read the poem several more times, inviting students to join in as they feel comfortable doing so. The goal is for students to become so familiar with the poem that they can read it on their own. • Briefly discuss the meaning of the poem and any outstanding literary features that you can point out to students (e.g., alliteration, rhymes). • Select an activity from the lesson page to do with students. The phonemic awareness activity is an excellent choice for the first day because it relates to words from the poem, but it does not require students to have extensive knowledge of the poem.
Day 2	• Reread the poem to students as they follow along silently or in a whisper voice. Be sure to point to the words as they are read. Read the poem chorally with students several times. • Select an activity or two from the lesson page to do with students. Expand on phonics vocabulary, fluency, or comprehension concepts from the poem. • Have each student dictate a brief personal response to the poem. Write students' responses on the board or a sheet of chart paper. Read the responses with students several times over the next few days.
Day 3	• Read the poem chorally once or twice with students. Have students try reading the poem on their own or with a partner. Ask students to read the poem several times, pointing to the words as they read. Observe students and provide encouragement as they read on their own. • Select an activity or two from the lesson page to do with students. Expand on phonics, vocabulary, fluency, or comprehension concepts from the poem. Provide students with the accompanying activity page if applicable.

<table>
<tr><th>Day</th><th>Suggested Instructional Plan</th></tr>
<tr><td>Day 4</td><td>
<ul>
<li>Pair students again (or have them work in trios or quartets) and have them read the poem to each other. Or refer to the Fluency section of the lesson plan for additional ideas for reading the poem.</li>
<li>Distribute copies of the Word Study activity sheet. Start with the rimes or word families from the poem that have been selected for this activity. In the chart, show students the word part, and write words that can be made from the word families. Once students write the words, have them practice reading them.</li>
<li>Have students use the words from the Word Building activity to complete the sentences activity. Have students try to read the sentences. If they are not yet able to do so, read the sentences with them. Students should then choose the correct word that goes in the appropriate blank. A Word Bank is provided to assist students with this section.</li>
</ul>
</td></tr>
<tr><td>Day 5</td><td>
<ul>
<li>Have students read the poem to you, individually or as a group. After several poems have been covered, allow students to choose poems from previous weeks to perform for the class. Complete any other activities from the lesson plan that you wish to do with students.</li>
<li>Have students refer to the Word Study activity sheet they have completed. Create a list of all the word family words that students created in the Word Building activity. Write each word on a 3" x 5" index card. Place the cards in a pocket chart. Have students practice reading the words.</li>
<li>Rearrange the word cards so that students focus their attention on the words and are not reading them from practice and memory. Also, feel free to add words from previous lessons for this activity.</li>
<li>Sort the words into various piles by their sounds—at the beginning, middle, or end of the words. For example, find all words that begin with the /b/ sound and put them in one pile.</li>
<li>Play word games, such as Memory. Make a duplicate set of word cards, turn both sets over, and have students try to match them, saying the words as they turn them over.</li>
<li>Above all, have fun with the poems. Help students find enjoyment in the rhyme, expression, and cadence found in reading rhythmical words aloud.</li>
</ul>
</td></tr>
</table>

Standards Correlations

Shell Education is committed to producing educational materials that are research and standards based. In this effort, we have correlated all of our products to the academic standards of all 50 states, the District of Columbia, and the Department of Defense Dependent Schools.

How to Find Standards Correlations

To print a customized correlation report of this product for your state, visit our website at **www.shelleducation.com** and follow the on-screen directions. If you require assistance in printing correlation reports, please contact Customer Service at 1-877-777-3450.

Purpose and Intent of Standards

The No Child Left Behind legislation mandates that all states adopt academic standards that identify the skills students will learn in kindergarten through grade twelve. While many states had already adopted academic standards prior to NCLB, the legislation set requirements to ensure the standards were detailed and comprehensive.

Standards are designed to focus instruction and guide adoption of curricula. Standards are statements that describe the criteria necessary for students to meet specific academic goals. They define the knowledge, skills, and content students should acquire at each level. Standards are also used to develop standardized tests to evaluate students' academic progress.

Teachers are required to demonstrate how their lessons meet state standards. State standards are used in development of all of our products, so educators can be assured they meet the academic requirements of each state.

McREL Compendium

We use the Mid-continent Research for Education and Learning (McREL) Compendium to create standards correlations. Each year, McREL analyzes state standards and revises the compendium. By following this procedure, McREL is able to produce a general compilation of national standards. Each lesson in this product is based on one or more McREL standards. The chart on the following pages list each standard taught in this product and the page numbers of the corresponding lessons.

Standards Correlation Chart

The chart below correlates the activities in *The Poet and the Professor: Poems for Building Reading Skills* with the McREL Content Knowledge.

Standards for Language Arts Grades K–2

Standards	Benchmarks	Lesson
Uses the general skills and strategies of the writing process	1.6 Uses writing and other methods to describe familiar persons, places, objects, or experiences	1, 6, 7, 9, 11, 16, 19, 21, 24, 25
	1.8 Writes for different purposes	6, 7, 9, 11, 14, 21, 24, 25
Uses the stylistic and rhetorical aspects of writing	2.1 Uses descriptive words to convey basic ideas	9, 11, 14, 16, 19, 21, 24, 25
Uses grammatical and mechanical conventions in written compositions	3.1 Uses conventions of print in writing	All
	3.2 Uses complete sentences in written compositions	All
	3.7 Uses conventions of spelling in written compositions	6, 7, 9, 11, 14, 16, 19, 21, 24, 25
	3.8 Uses conventions of capitalization in written compositions	6, 7, 9, 11, 14, 16, 19, 21, 24, 25
	3.9 Uses conventions of punctuation in written compositions	6, 7, 9, 11, 14, 16, 19, 21, 24, 25
Uses the general skills and strategies of the reading process	5.3 Uses basic elements of phonetic analysis	All
	5.6 Understands level-appropriate sight words and vocabulary	1, 4, 5, 7, 8, 10, 11, 12, 13, 15, 17, 18, 20, 21, 22, 25, 26, 28
	5.8 Reads aloud familiar stories, poems, and passages with fluency and expression	All
Uses reading skills and strategies to understand and interpret a variety of literary texts	6.1 Uses reading skills and strategies to understand a variety of familiar literary passages and texts	3, 4, 5, 7, 8, 10, 14, 27, 28
	6.3 Knows setting, main characters, main events, sequence, and problems in stories	4, 10, 13, 15, 19
	6.5 Relates stories to personal experiences	2, 6, 10, 11, 13, 16, 23, 26, 29, 30
Uses listening and speaking skills for different purposes	8.1 Makes contributions in class and group discussions	All
	8.2 Asks and responds to questions	All
	8.5 Uses level-appropriate vocabulary in speech	1, 9, 13, 17, 21, 22, 25
	8.5 Recites and responds to familiar stories, poems, and rhymes with patterns	1, 2, 6, 10, 13, 22, 23, 28, 29, 30

Activity Skill—Correlation Chart

McREL Content Knowledge Standards for Grades K–2

Activity Page	Standards-Based Skill or Focus	Page
Phonemic Awareness		
Beginning or Ending Sound?	Identifying Phoneme Position	18
Ick!	Phoneme Identity	54
Shhhhh!	Initial and Ending Phoneme Identity	86
Ends Like Me	Phoneme Identity	106
A Handful of Rhymes	Phoneme Categorization	122
Begins the Same	Phoneme Identity	126
Phonics		
Long O	Spelling Pattern *–ow*	38
Make New Words	Identifying Initial and Medial Sounds	66
Short or Long *A*?	Long and Short *A*	70
Spelling Long *I*	Long *I* Spelling Patterns	114
Compound Words	Compound Words	118
Add *-ed*	Past Tense Words	130
Vocabulary		
Labeling a Diagram	Categorizing—Clothing	22
Categories	Categorizing—Food	26
Wild or Tame?	Word Meaning	42
-otion Words	Word Meaning	46
Describing Color	Color Words	94
Where in the World?	Global Locations	110
Fluency		
Sight and Color Words	Recognizing Sight and Color Words	34
To the Tune Of	Reading with Rhythm, Flow, and Meter	58
How Does It End?	Reading with Intonation	62
Pause Please	Reading with Rhythm, Flow, and Meter	78
Pickles Graph	Word Recognition	82
Number Words	Number Word Recognition	98
Comprehension		
Show the Order	Sequencing	30
Playing Games	Text-to-Self Connection	50
What Is Happening?	Text Comprehension	74
Sequence the Poem	Sequencing	90
Place It in the Toy Box	Text Comprehension	102
Summer Fun	Text-to-Self Connection	134

About the Poets

Dr. Timothy Rasinski, Ph.D, is a Professor of Education in the Reading and Writing Center at Kent State University, Ohio, where he directs the reading clinic. His scholarly interests include reading fluency, word study, reading in the elementary and middle grades, and readers who struggle. He has served on the Board of Directors of the International Reading Association and is widely published in reading journals. His book *The Fluent Reader* provides background information and practical applications for the teaching of fluency. Dr. Rasinski speaks all over the country to education audiences about reading fluency. His research on fluency has been cited by the National Reading Panel and was influential in having fluency included as one of the five essential components of reading instruction in the Reading First legislation.

Karen McGuigan Brothers recently retired from the Reading and Writing Development Center at Kent State University, Kent, Ohio. For nearly 30 years, she served as the liaison for parents and teachers inquiring about participation in the Center's testing and tutoring programs in reading and also coordinated the development of those programs. Through exposure to children's literature at the Center, as well as her experience as a mother and grandmother, she became familiar with what subject matter appeals to children and incorporates that into her poetry. In addition to co-authoring *The Poet and the Professor: Poems for Building Reading Skills*, she has written children's poems for numerous other publications.

Summer's Over

See pages 10–11 for ideas to introduce the poem. Complete some or all of the following activities throughout the week. The activities on this page may be completed before, during, or after reading the poem. Select activities based on your students' needs.

Phonemic Awareness

- Ask students what sound they hear at the beginning of the word *summer's*. Have students identify the other word in the poem that has the /s/ sound at the beginning of the word (school).
- Have students name words that have the /s/ sound at the end of the word. Chart students' responses.
- Distribute copies of page 18.
- Have students identify the position of the /s/ sound in each word by filling in the first or second bubble.

Phonics

- Write the words *pool*, *cool*, and *rule* on the board or on a sheet of chart paper. Have students identify the letters that make the /o͞o/ sound. Discuss the two different spelling patterns.
- Ask students to practice spelling the following words with the *-oo* spelling pattern: *tool*, *fool*, and *school*.

Vocabulary

- Ask students to define the word *rule*. Are there other definitions with which they are familiar?
- Discuss with students the phrase *teachers rule*. How do teachers rule? Who rules during the summertime?

Fluency

- Divide the class into groups of four. Assign each student in the groups a different pair of lines from the poem. Provide sufficient time for each student to practice his or her lines and for the group to practice reciting the poem together.
- Have groups of students take turns performing the poem for the rest of the class.

Comprehension

- Have each student fold a sheet of construction paper in half. One half should be labeled *Summer*, the other half, *School*. Discuss activities in which students participate during each category.
- Ask students to draw pictures depicting the activities they listed.

Word Study Extension

Use page 19 to extend word concepts from the poem.

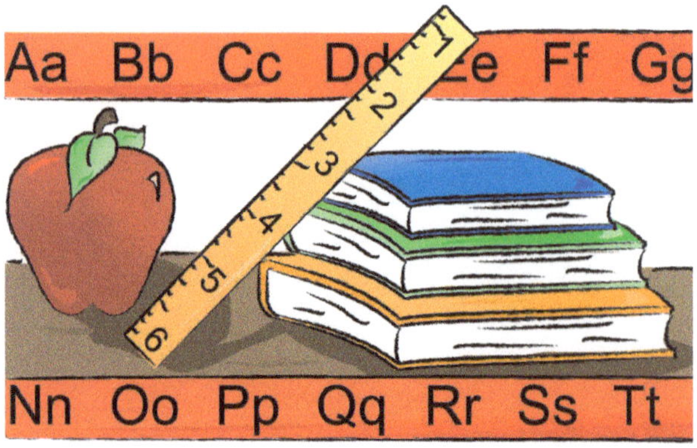

Summer's Over

Summer's over.
Close the pool.
Summer's over.
Time for school.
Summer's over.
Books are cool.
Summer's over.
Teachers rule!

—Tim Rasinski

Name:______________________

Beginning or Ending Sound?

Directions: Say the name of each picture. Fill in the first bubble if you hear /s/ at the beginning of the word. Fill in the second bubble if you hear /s/ at the end of the word.

1.

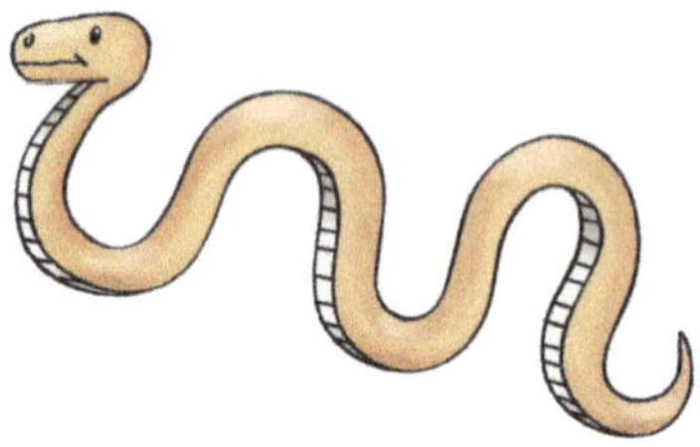

2.

3.

4.

5.

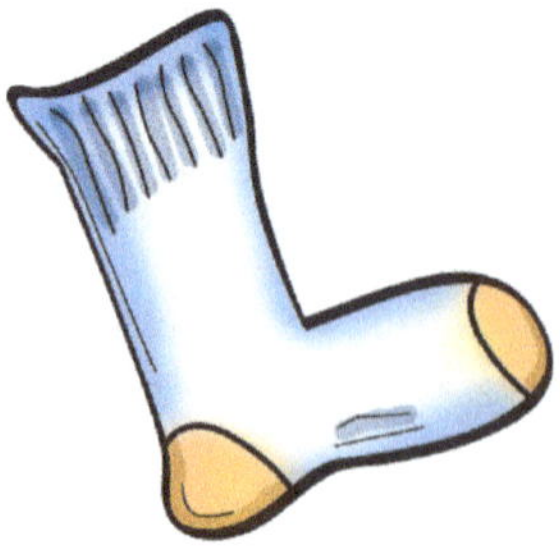

6.

7.

8.

9.

Name:________________________

Word Building

I. Directions: Write words from the poem in the correct groups. Then add new words to each group.

Words with *-ool*	**Words with *-ook***	**Words About Summer Fun**

II. Directions: Read each sentence. Write the missing word. Use the Word Bank for help.

1. Our teacher has a lot of ____________________.

2. I like to swim in our ____________________.

3. My mom says I ____________________ like her.

4. I go to ____________________ every day.

Word Bank

pool school look books

I'm Ready

See pages 10–11 for ideas to introduce the poem. Complete some or all of the following activities throughout the week. The activities on this page may be completed before, during, or after reading the poem. Select activities based on your students' needs.

Phonemic Awareness

- Tell students you are going to say a word very slowly, one sound at a time. Have students blend the sounds together to make a word. Say /sh/, /o͞o/, /z/—*shoes*. Students should respond with *shoes*.
- Practice with the words listed below:

  /h/, /ă/, /t/—*hat*

  /c/, /o͞o/, /l/—*cool*

Phonics

- Write the words *new*, *blue*, and *shoe* on the board or on a sheet of chart paper. Identify the letters in each word that make the /o͞o/ sound. Discuss the different spelling patterns.
- Tell students that when the /o͞o/ sound is at the end of a word, it is more commonly spelled with the *-ue* or *-ew* spelling pattern.
- Tell students to practice spelling the following words: *glue*, *true*, *clue*, *due*, *chew*, *flew*, and *blew*.
- Ask students to think of other words that rhyme with *blue*. Write students' responses on the board or on a sheet of chart paper. Identify the various spelling patterns that can be seen in these words (e.g., *two*, *moo*, and *view*).

Vocabulary

- Distribute copies of page 22.
- Discuss with students the articles of clothing the boy in the picture is wearing. Ask students to label the clothing. Encourage students to think of other clothing items.

Fluency

- Ask students how they feel about going back to school after summer vacation.
- Practice reading the poem with the different tones students mentioned (e.g., excited, scared, happy, sad).

Comprehension

- Have students brainstorm what they do to get ready to go back to school. Create a list on the board or on a sheet of chart paper.
- Have students place a tally mark on the list beside each thing they did when they were getting ready for this school year. Compare the list the class creates with the description in the poem.

Word Study Extension

Use page 23 to extend word concepts from the poem.

I'm Ready

I got new jeans.
I got new shoes.
I got new shirts
In greens and blues.
I got a new hat.
I'm looking real cool.
Now I'm ready for
The first day of school!

—Karen McGuigan Brothers

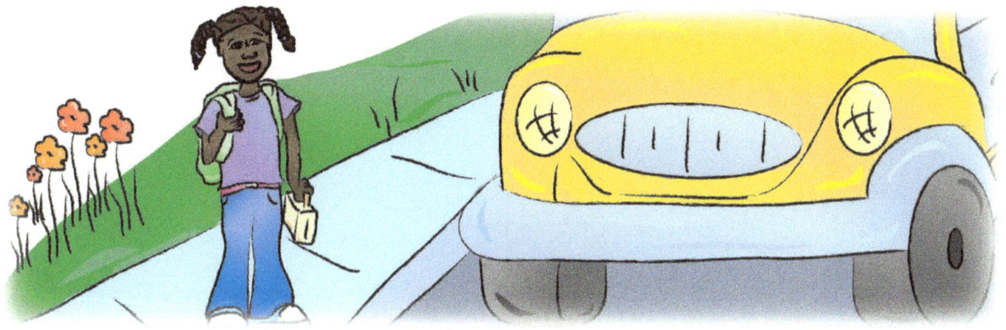

Name: ______________________

Labeling a Diagram

Directions: Use words from the Word Bank to label the clothing items below.

Word Bank

jeans
shirt
shoes
hat
belt
jacket

1. ______________
2. ______________

3. ______________
4. ______________
5. ______________
6. ______________

Think of two more clothing items. Draw a picture of each and label each with its name.

Name: ____________________

Word Building

I. Directions: Write words from the poem in the correct groups. Then add new words to each group.

Words with *-ool*	Words with *-ot*	Words About the First Day of School

II. Directions: Read each sentence. Write the missing word. Use the Word Bank for help.

1. My little brother is a ____________________.

2. In fall the weather turns ____________________.

3. The ____________________ is filled with water.

4. I have a ____________________ of friends.

Word Bank

lot tot cool pool

The Sun's Glow

See pages 10–11 for ideas to introduce the poem. Complete some or all of the following activities throughout the week. The activities on this page may be completed before, during, or after reading the poem. Select activities based on your students' needs.

Phonemic Awareness

- Tell students you will be saying two words. If the words end with the same sound, students should smile. If the words do not end with the same sound, they should frown. Say the words *see* and *glee*. Students should respond by smiling.
- Continue with the words below:

  grow/mow—(smile)

  show/bow—(smile)

  slow/slide—(frown)

  low/snow—(smile)

Phonics

- Write the words *grow, glow, tow,* and *crow* on the board or on a sheet of chart paper. Have students review the list and identify the spelling pattern that occurs in all four words. Students should indicate that the /ō/ sound at the end of a word is spelled *-ow*.
- Say the rhyming words that end in the *-ow* spelling pattern from the phonemic awareness activity. Have students write the words, practicing the *-ow* spelling pattern.

Vocabulary

- Ask each student to name his or her favorite vegetable. Discuss the characteristics of a vegetable.
- Distribute copies of page 26.
- Tell students to cut out the food picture cards at the bottom of the page and glue each card in the correct column.

Fluency

- Echo-read the poem with students. Read the first two lines of the poem out loud. Have students repeat after you.
- Ask students to try to match your voice intonation. Continue reading pairs of lines out loud and have students echo back. Repeat the activity. This time, select a student to read the poem and have the rest of the class echo him or her.

Comprehension

- Encourage discussion about the following lines from the poem:

  "Under the sun's nurturing glow."

  "It's nature's number one hit show!"
- Divide students into two groups and assign each group a line to discuss. After a few minutes, have the group discuss the opposite line. Come back together as a class to discuss the lines.

Word Study Extension

Use page 27 to extend word concepts from the poem.

The Sun's Glow

Corn, carrots, and cabbage grow
Under the sun's nurturing glow.
Some grow fast and some grow slow.
It's nature's number one hit show!

—Tim Rasinski

Name: ______________________

Categories

Directions: Cut out the food picture cards at the bottom of the page. Glue the picture cards in the correct column.

Vegetable	Not a Vegetable

cheese

apple

carrot

milk

corn

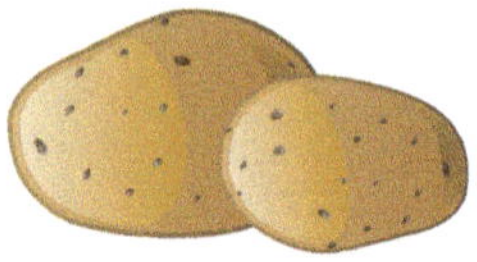

potatoes

egg

peas

Name:____________________

Word Building

I. Directions: Write words from the poem in the correct groups. Then add new words to each group.

Words with *-and*	Words with *-ast*	Words About Gardens

II. Directions: Read each sentence. Write the missing word. Use the Word Bank for help.

1. The doctor put a ________________ on my broken arm.
2. I play trumpet in the ________________.
3. I was the ________________ one to finish.
4. I love to play in the ________________ on the beach.

Word Bank

sand cast band last

Roller Coaster

See pages 10–11 for ideas to introduce the poem. Complete some or all of the following activities throughout the week. The activities on this page may be completed before, during, or after reading the poem. Select activities based on your students' needs.

Phonemic Awareness

- Ask students what sound they hear at the end of the word *track*. Students should respond with the /k/ sound.
- Say the words below, one at a time. Have students show a thumbs-up sign if the word ends with the same sound as the word *track*. Students should show a thumbs-down sign if the word does not end with the same sound as the word *track*.

  coaster—(thumbs-down)

  back—(thumbs-up)

  drop—(thumbs-down)

Phonics

- Emphasize the spelling of the /k/ sound at the end of words with the letters *-ck*. Write the words *track, back,* and *clack* on the board or on a sheet of chart paper. Underline the letters *-ck* at the end of each word.
- Ask students to think of other words that end with the /k/ sound. Write students' responses on the board or on a sheet of chart paper, emphasizing the *-ck* spelling pattern when appropriate.

Vocabulary

- Write the following two definitions of the word *track* on the board:

  track—footprints left by animals or people

  track—rails on which something runs
- Ask students which definition best fits the word *track* used in the poem. Have students create sentences to show their understanding of both the definitions.

Fluency

- Pair students and have them brainstorm methods to read the words *drop* and *whoosh* as if they were making the sounds associated with the words.
- Ask each pair of students to share the sounds they created with the class. As a group, determine the way in which the words should be read. Then reread the poem, having students read those words in the chosen way.

Comprehension

- Distribute copies of page 30.
- Discuss the sequence of events in the poem. Have students show the sequence of events in the poem by gluing the sentence strips in the correct order.

Word Study Extension

Use page 31 to extend word concepts from the poem.

Roller Coaster

The roller coaster
Climbs up the track.
First I look down,
And then I look back.

We reach the top,
And then we drop.
Whoosh to the bottom,
I'm glad to stop!

—Karen McGuigan Brothers

Name:________________________

Show the Order

Directions: Cut out the sentence strips at the bottom of the page. Think about the sequence of events in the poem. Glue the sentence strips in the correct order in the chart below.

1.
2.
3.
4.

The roller coaster goes down the track.

I look all around.

The roller coaster goes up the track.

The roller coaster gets to the top.

Name:________________________

Word Building

I. Directions: Write words from the poem in the correct groups. Then add new words to each group.

Words with *-ack*	Words with *-op*	Words About Roller Coasters

II. Directions: Read each sentence. Write the missing word. Use the Word Bank for help.

1. When his mom called, ________________ went home.
2. The car ________________ in front of my house.
3. I carry my books in a ________________.
4. The ________________ was closed after school.

Word Bank

stopped Jack pack shop

Frozen Treats

See pages 10–11 for ideas to introduce the poem. Complete some or all of the following activities throughout the week. The activities on this page may be completed before, during, or after reading the poem. Select activities based on your students' needs.

Phonemic Awareness

- Read the words from the list below, one at a time. Have students identify words that end with the *-ick* spelling pattern. Students can indicate the words that end with *-ick* by rubbing their stomach. If the words do not end with *-ick*, students should do nothing.

kick	*pot*	*stick*
rock	*pick*	*back*

- Read only the words from the list that end with the *-ick* spelling pattern. Have students segment each word by saying one sound at a time. For example, with the word *kick*, say /k/, /ĭ/, /k/.

Phonics

- Write the word *yellow* on the board or on a sheet of chart paper. Ask students to identify which letters are doubled in the word. Students should respond with the letters *ll*.
- Tell students that if the word *yellow* is segmented, the double letters (*ll*) make only one sound. List the following words below on the board or on a sheet of chart paper and ask students to practice reading them.

daddy	*shell*	*call*
letter	*butter*	*doggy*

Vocabulary

- Tell students that you will be writing some sentences. They are to determine which sentence has the same meaning of the word *treat* that is used in the poem.
- Write the following sentences on the board:

  We have to *treat* adults with respect. (no)

  Mom gave me a *treat* when I got home from school. (yes)

  The doctor will *treat* the baby for the flu. (no)

Fluency

- Distribute copies of page 34.
- Ask students to trace the color words with the matching colors and the sight words with a pencil. Read the poem together. Students will be able to recognize the words more easily.

Comprehension

- Have students brainstorm different types of frozen treats. List students' responses on the board or on a sheet of chart paper.
- Ask students to identify the color(s) of each treat and whether or not it is on a stick. Reread the poem. Compare the class list with the poem.

Word Study Extension

Use page 35 to extend word concepts from the poem.

Frozen Treats

Frozen treat upon a stick.
Frozen treat for me to lick.
Red or yellow, take your pick.
Starts to melt, so eat it quick!

—Karen McGuigan Brothers

Name:____________________________

Sight and Color Words

Directions: Trace the color words with the matching crayon color. Trace the sight words with a pencil. Practice reading the poem.

Frozen Treats

Frozen treats upon a stick.

Frozen treats for me to lick.

Red or yellow, take your pick.

Starts to melt, so eat it quick!

Name: ____________________

Word Building

I. Directions: Write words from the poem in the correct groups. Then add new words to each group.

Words with *-ick*	Words with *-eat*	Words About Treats

II. Directions: Read each sentence. Write the missing word. Use the Word Bank for help.

1. The ice made the road ____________________.
2. The music had a good ____________________.
3. I was ____________________ with a cold.
4. Dogs like to eat ____________________.

Word Bank

sick slick beat meat

The Night-light

See pages 10–11 for ideas to introduce the poem. Complete some or all of the following activities throughout the week. The activities on this page may be completed before, during, or after reading the poem. Select activities based on your students' needs.

Phonemic Awareness

- Tell students that you are going to say a sound and a word. Ask them to tell you the new word that is made when you add the sound to the beginning of the word. Tell students to add the /g/ sound to the word *low*. Students should respond with *glow*.
- Continue with the words below:

  Add /s/ to *care—scare*

  Add /d/ to *ark—dark*

  Add /r/ to *ice—rice*

Phonics

- Ask students which vowel sound they hear in the words *glow, know, low,* and *slow* (/ō/). Write each word on the board or on a sheet of chart paper. Emphasize the *-ow* spelling pattern in each word.
- Distribute copies of page 38.
- Have students practice spelling words with the /ō/ sound at the end of the word.

Vocabulary

- Discuss the phrase "I'm feeling low" with students. What does it mean to feel low? What does it mean to feel great?
- Create a two-column chart on the board or on a sheet of chart paper. Label the left side of the chart "Feeling Low." Label the right side of the chart "Feeling Great." Ask students to name things that make them feel low and great. Write students' responses in the appropriate column.

Fluency

- Divide students into groups of three or four. Ask each group to create facial expressions or gestures that match the poem.
- Ask students to practice reading the poem several times while doing the actions. Then allow each group to perform the poem for the rest of the class.

Comprehension

- Ask students why night-lights are used. What part of a night-light would burn out? What would happen if the lightbulb burned out?
- Encourage students to write a story using the title of the poem. The story can relate to the poem or it can relate to a new theme.

Word Study Extension

Use page 39 to extend word concepts from the poem.

The Night-light

Though the moon is out
And there's a glow,
I'm scared of the dark!
Didn't you know?
My night-light is out,
And I'm feeling low.
So, find a new bulb,
And don't be slow.

—Tim Rasinski

Name:______________________

Long *O*

Directions: Say the name of each picture. Complete each sentence by writing the name of the long /ō/ word to match the picture.

1. 	She wore a ____________________ in her hair.
2. 	He had to ____________________ the lawn.
3. 	Dad can ____________________ a boat.
4. 	We will ____________________ the broken car.
5. 	Tim knows how to ____________________ bubbles.

Name: ______________________

Word Building

I. Directions: Write words from the poem in the correct groups. Then add new words to each group.

Words with *-ow*	Words with *-ark*	Words About the Night

II. Directions: Read each sentence. Write the missing word. Use the Word Bank for help.

1. Cats purr and dogs ______________________.
2. The ______________________ of the moon was bright.
3. My best friend's name is ______________________.
4. Mom says I'm a ______________________-off.

Word Bank

Mark bark glow show

Call Their Name

See pages 10–11 for ideas to introduce the poem. Complete some or all of the following activities throughout the week. The activities on this page may be completed before, during, or after reading the poem. Select activities based on your students' needs.

Phonemic Awareness

- Tell students that you are going to say a word very slowly, one sound at a time. Have students blend the sounds together to make a word. Say /t/, /ā/, /m/. Students should respond with *tame*.
- Practice with the words listed below:

  /s/, /ā/, /m/—*same*

  /sh/, /ā/, /m/—*shame*

  /c/, /ā/, /m/—*came*

Phonics

- Write the words *tame, same, shame, came,* and *name* on the board or on a sheet of chart paper. Repeat the phonemic awareness activity, this time asking students to count how many sounds they hear in each word.
- Encourage students to compare the number of sounds to the number of letters in each word. Ask students which letter is not represented by a sound. Relate the /ā/ sound in each word to the silent *e* at the end of each word.
- Ask students to help you spell the following words: *blame, fame,* and *game*.

Vocabulary

- Discuss the words *wild* and *tame*. As a class, brainstorm definitions and examples of each word.
- Distribute copies of page 42.
- Have students circle the word *tame* if the animal is probably tame like a pet. Have students circle the word *wild* if the animal is probably wild and not a pet.

Fluency

- Echo-read the poem several times with students. Read the first line of the poem while students listen. Then have students read the line.
- Continue reading and echoing each line of the poem. As you notice students who are able to read the poem on their own, give them the opportunity to be the "teacher" and have the rest of the class echo them.

Comprehension

- Ask each student to draw a picture of what his or her home would look like at the end of the poem if "they all came when I called their name."
- Ask students to write about what they would do to get the animals out of their homes.

Word Study Extension

Use page 43 to extend word concepts from the poem.

Call Their Name

Wolves are wild,
And dogs are tame.
Lions and tigers
Are about the same.

I'd be surprised,
It'd be a shame,
If they all came,
When I called their name.

—Tim Rasinski

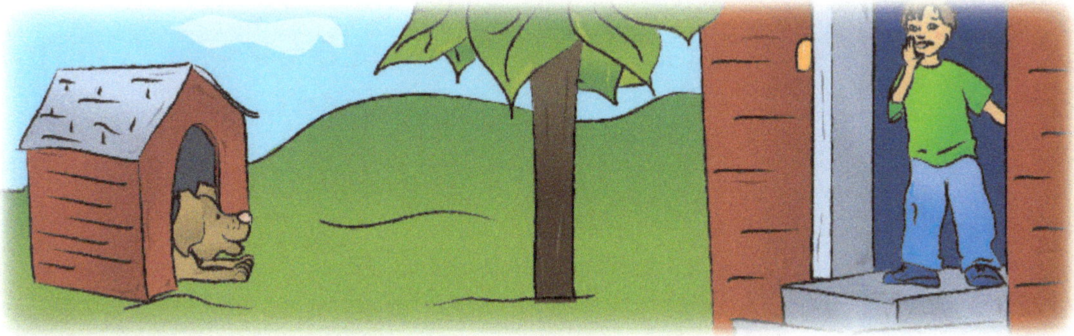

Name:________________________

Wild or Tame?

Directions: Look at each animal. Circle the word *tame* if the animal is probably tame like a pet. Circle the word *wild* if the animal is probably wild and not a pet.

1.  tame wild	**2.**  tame wild
3.  tame wild	**4.**  tame wild
5.  tame wild	**6.**  tame wild
7.  tame wild	**8.**  tame wild

Name: ______________________

Word Building

I. Directions: Write words from the poem in the correct groups. Then add new words to each group.

Words with *-ame*	Words with *-ild*	Words About Animals

II. Directions: Read each sentence. Write the missing word. Use the Word Bank for help.

1. ______________________ animals live in the jungle.

2. My dad ______________________ home after work.

3. His bike is the ______________________ as mine.

4. A two-year-old is a ______________________.

Word Bank

Wild same came child

A Simple Notion

See pages 10–11 for ideas to introduce the poem. Complete some or all of the following activities throughout the week. The activities on this page may be completed before, during, or after reading the poem. Select activities based on your students' needs.

Phonemic Awareness

- Say the words *super* and *smart* to students. Ask students if the words begin with the same sound.
- Tell students you are going to say two words. If the two words begin with the same sound, they are to show you a thumbs-up sign. If the two words do not begin with the same sound, they are to show you a thumbs-down sign.
- Practice with the words below:

  very/visitors—(thumbs-up)

  roly/poly—(thumbs-down)

  two/turkeys—(thumbs-up)

Phonics

- Write the word *lotion* on the board or on a sheet of chart paper. Identify the letters *tion* as the letters that sound like "shun" at the end of the word.
- Ask students to identify other words in the poem that have the same sound and spelling pattern. Brainstorm other words that have the same sound. Write students' responses on the board or on a sheet of chart paper.

Vocabulary

- Distribute copies of page 46.
- Discuss the definitions of the words *notion*, *motion*, and *commotion*. Ask students to read each sentence and decide if it describes a notion, motion, or commotion.

Fluency

- Divide the class into two groups. Assign one group to read the even-numbered lines and the other group to read the odd-numbered lines. Read the poem with the groups alternating lines.
- Ask the groups of students to change roles and read the poem again.

Comprehension

- Have each student design an advertisement for "Super-Smart Lotion." Included in the design should be what the lotion is for and how to use it.
- Encourage students to draw an advertisement or create a commercial that can be performed in front of the class. Ask students to use ideas from the poem in their advertisements.

Word Study Extension

Use page 47 to extend word concepts from the poem.

A Simple Notion

Here's an idea—
It's a simple notion.
Let's invent
A smart-making lotion.
Rub your head
In a circular motion.
Your super brain
Will cause a commotion!

—Tim Rasinski

Name: ____________________

-otion Words

Directions: Look at the box below for the definitions of a notion, motion, and commotion. Read each sentence. On the line, write the word that best describes the sentence.

notion—an idea
motion—movement
commotion—a noisy disturbance

1. We yelled, "Surprise!" when she walked in the room. ____________________

2. The roller coaster began to climb the hill. ____________________

3. Let's eat first. Then we can play outside. ____________________

4. The boys were arguing about whose turn it was. ____________________

5. We can work on the puzzle together. ____________________

6. The wheels on the bike began to turn. ____________________

Name: ____________________

Word Building

I. Directions: Write words from the poem in the correct groups. Then add new words to each group.

Words with *-otion*	Words with *-ent*	Words About Being Smart

II. Directions: Read each sentence. Write the missing word. Use the Word Bank for help.

1. I wish I had a magic ____________________.

2. We ____________________ to the ball game.

3. The ____________________ of the boat made me ill.

4. On vacation, we slept in a ____________________.

Word Bank

potion went motion tent

Video Game

See pages 10–11 for ideas to introduce the poem. Complete some or all of the following activities throughout the week. The activities on this page may be completed before, during, or after reading the poem. Select activities based on your students' needs.

Phonemic Awareness

- Tell students you are going to say a word very slowly, one sound at a time. Have students blend the sounds together to make a word.
- Say /g/, /ā/, /m/. Students should respond with *game*.
- Practice with the words listed below:
  /s/, /ā/, /m/—*same*
  /w/, /ī/, /l/, /d/—*wild*
  /n/, /ĕ/, /v/, /er/—*never*

Phonics

- Write the words *same, game,* and *tame* on the board or on a sheet of chart paper. Have students identify the vowels in each word.
- Tell students that in an *a_e* spelling pattern, usually the *e* is silent and the *a* has a long vowel sound. Circle the *e* at the end of each word and draw an arrow to the *a* in each word.
- Ask students to practice spelling the following words with the same spelling pattern: *cake, late, made, cage,* and *tape.*

Vocabulary

- Discuss the words *wild* and *tame.* Reference the poem "Call Their Name" (page 41) if you have already read it.
- Ask students to identify wild and tame animals. Discuss how a video game could be wild or tame.

Fluency

- Pair students to practice reading the poem together. One student can read the odd-numbered lines and the other student can read the even-numbered lines.
- Encourage students to practice reading the poem several times so they read it as if only one person were reading it. Encourage the student reading the word *wild* to read it as if he or she were wild. Encourage the student reading the word *tame* to read it as if he or she were tame.

Comprehension

- Distribute copies of page 50.
- Tell students to list five words they think of when playing a wild video game and list five words they think of when playing a tame video game.
- Tell students to write about which type of game they would prefer to play. Encourage students to use words from the appropriate list in their writing. Have them share their writing with partners or with the class.

Word Study Extension

Use page 51 to extend word concepts from the poem.

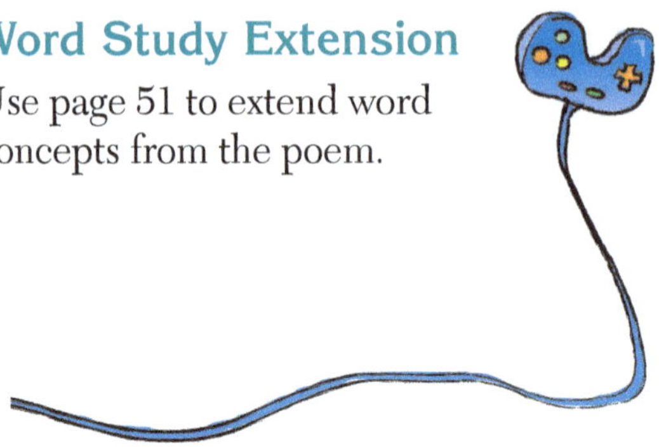

Video Game

My video game
Is never the same.
Sometimes it's wild
And sometimes it's tame.

—Karen McGuigan Brothers

Name: ______________________

Playing Games

Directions: Think about playing a video game that is wild. Think about playing a video game that is tame. List five words below that you think describe each game. Then write about whether you would rather play a wild video game or a tame one. Use the words from the list in your writing.

Wild Video Game	Tame Video Game
1.	1.
2.	2.
3.	3.
4.	4.
5.	5.

____

____

____

____

____

____

____

Name: ______________________

Word Building

I. Directions: Write words from the poem in the correct groups. Then add new words to each group.

Words with *-ame*	Words with *-y*	Words About Games

II. Directions: Read each sentence. Write the missing word. Use the Word Bank for help.

1. ______________________ little sister is in kindergarten.

2. Dogs and cats are ______________________ animals.

3. Our teacher tells us to ______________________ our best.

4. My friend and I have the ______________________ first name.

Word Bank

try same tame My

Tasty Treats

See pages 10–11 for ideas to introduce the poem. Complete some or all of the following activities throughout the week. The activities on this page may be completed before, during, or after reading the poem. Select activities based on your students' needs.

Phonemic Awareness

- Tell students that you are going to say a word and then ask them to change the beginning sound to make a new word. Say the word *pick*. Have students change the /p/ in *pick* to /s/. Students should respond with *sick*.
- Practice with the words listed below:

  Change the /s/ in *sick* to /t/—*tick*

  Change the /t/ in *tick* to /k/—*kick*

  Change the /k/ in *kick* to /l/—*lick*
- Distribute copies of page 54.
- Have students say the name of each picture. Students should color the picture if it ends the same way as the word *kick*.

Phonics

- Write the words *cream* and *treat* on the board or on a sheet of chart paper. Underline the vowels *ea* that make the /ē/ sound in each word. Add the following words and have a volunteer underline the *ea* spelling pattern in each word: *meal, beak, dream, please, meat,* and *eat*.
- Ask students to practice reading each word. Then cover up the words and have students practice spelling each word.

Vocabulary

- Discuss the word *sick* with students. Have students identify different ways a person can be sick.
- Ask students if they think the way the word is used in the poem means "sick with the flu" or "sick with a tummy ache." How can they tell? What clues are given in the poem to help the reader decide?

Fluency

- Model reading the poem, pausing in the appropriate places and at the end of each line.
- Tell students to practice reading the poem to a partner. Encourage them to pause for an appropriate amount of time as they read. Then invite volunteers to recite the poem in front of the class.

Comprehension

- Ask students if they have ever eaten so much that they felt sick. What did they eat? Discuss the lesson they can learn from their experiences and from the poem.
- Ask each student to draw a picture and write about how to make a good choice when presented with many food options.

Word Study Extension

Use page 55 to extend word concepts from the poem.

Tasty Treats

A hot dog on a stick—
Now that's a tasty treat.
An ice cream cone to lick—
Give me one to eat.
So many snacks to pick,
So much for me to eat.
Too much makes me sick!
I'd better take a seat.

—Karen McGuigan Brothers

Name: ______________________

Ick!

Directions: Say the name of each picture. Color the picture if it ends the same way as the word *pick*.

1.

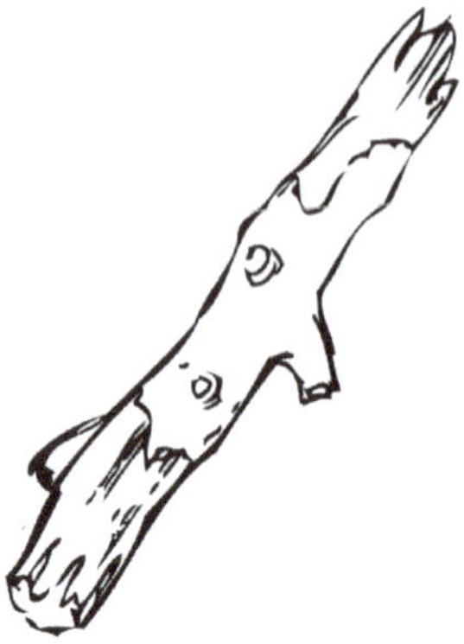

2.

3.

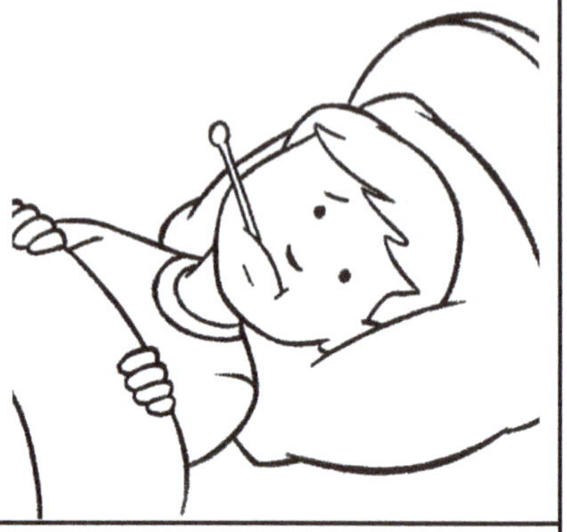

4.

5.

6.

7.

8.

9.

Name: ______________________

Word Building

I. Directions: Write words from the poem in the correct groups. Then add new words to each group.

Words with *-ick*	**Words with *-eat***	**Words About Treats**

II. Directions: Read each sentence. Write the missing word. Use the Word Bank for help.

1. I like to ______________________ lollipops.

2. The sun makes ______________________ for us.

3. Dad let me ______________________ the color of our new car.

4. Hot dogs and hamburgers are my favorite ______________.

Word Bank

pick lick heat meats

Short or Tall?

See pages 10–11 for ideas to introduce the poem. Complete some or all of the following activities throughout the week. The activities on this page may be completed before, during, or after reading the poem. Select activities based on your students' needs.

Phonemic Awareness

- Have students identify the rhyming words in the poem. Point out that all of the rhyming words have the sound /all/ at the end of the word. Brainstorm other words that have the /all/ sound at the end of the word. Write students' responses on the board or on a sheet of chart paper.
- Have students change the vowel sound in the rhyming words to make new words. For example, tell students to change the /all/ in *tall* to /ell/. Students should respond with *tell*.
- Continue substituting the vowel sound in all of the rhyming words that were brainstormed. The new words can be silly or serious.

Phonics

- Point out how the letters *s* and *h* work together to make the /sh/ sound as in *short*. Have students brainstorm other words that have the /sh/ sound. Emphasize the *sh* spelling pattern as you write each word. Write students' responses on the board or on a sheet of chart paper.
- Once students are done brainstorming, ask them to identify whether the /sh/ sound is at the beginning, middle, or end of each word.

Vocabulary

- Discuss the definition of the words *short* and *tall* to compare height by adding *-er* and *-est* to the ends of the words.
- Compare objects in the room, using the terms *short* and *tall*. For example, "The bookcase is shorter than the door." Encourage students to compare objects.

Fluency

- Distribute copies of page 58.
- Have students practice singing the poem "Twinkle, Twinkle Little Star." Then ask them to practice singing the poem "Short or Tall?" to the same tune.

Comprehension

- Brainstorm reasons why it is useful to be tall and reasons why it is useful to be short. Write students' responses on the board or on a sheet of chart paper.
- Ask students to answer the question in the first line of the poem, *Are you short or are you tall?*, by writing a response and drawing a picture.

Word Study Extension

Use page 59 to extend word concepts from the poem.

Short or Tall?

Are you short or are you tall?
Can you jump to catch a ball
And reach high up on a wall—
Or really not too high at all?
Are you short or are you tall?
It doesn't matter much at all.

—Karen McGuigan Brothers

Name: ______________________

To the Tune Of

I. Directions: Practice reading the poem "Twinkle, Twinkle Little Star." Sing the song if you know the tune.

Twinkle, Twinkle Little Star

Twinkle, twinkle little star,
How I wonder what you are.
Up above the world so high,
Like a diamond in the sky.
Twinkle, twinkle little star,
How I wonder what you are.

II. Directions: Practice singing "Short or Tall?" to the tune of "Twinkle, Twinkle Little Star."

Short or Tall?

Are you short or are you tall?
Can you jump to catch a ball
And reach high up on a wall—
Or really not too high at all?
Are you short or are you tall?
It doesn't matter much at all.

—Karen McGuigan Brothers

Name: ____________________

Word Building

I. Directions: Write words from the poem in the correct groups. Then add new words to each group.

Words with *-all*	Words with *-ort*	Words About You

II. Directions: Read each sentence. Write the missing word. Use the Word Bank for help.

1. Baseball is a fun ____________________ to play.

2. Mom bought me clothes at the ____________________.

3. My friend is tall, but his brother is ____________________.

4. The horse is in a ____________________ in the barn.

Word Bank

short mall stall sport

Mouse in the House

See pages 10–11 for ideas to introduce the poem. Complete some or all of the following activities throughout the week. The activities on this page may be completed before, during, or after reading the poem. Select activities based on your students' needs.

Phonemic Awareness

- Tell students that you are going to say a word and then ask them to change the beginning sound to make a new word. Say the word *cat*. Have students change the /c/ in *cat* to /m/. Students should respond with *mat*.
- Practice with the words listed below:

  Change the /m/ in *mat* to /s/—*sat*

  Change the /s/ in *sat* to /h/—*hat*

  Change the /h/ in *hat* to /p/—*pat*

Phonics

- Write the words *mouse* and *house* on the board or on a sheet of chart paper. Underline the letters *ou*. Ask students to identify the sound these letters make in both words. Students should respond with /ow/.
- Add the words *how* and *cow* to the board or chart paper. Point out that when the sound /ow/ is in the middle of the word, it is sometimes spelled *ou* (e.g., *mouse*), and when the /ow/ sound is at the end of the word, it is sometimes spelled *ow* (e.g., *cow*, *how*). Have students brainstorm other words that fit each category.

Vocabulary

- Write the word *scat* on the board or on a sheet of chart paper.
- Encourage students to suggest other words that mean the same as *scat*. Reread the fifth line of the poem, replacing student-suggested words for the word *scat*.

Fluency

- Write a declarative sentence on the board or on a sheet of chart paper and have students practice reading it. Then change the ending mark to a question mark and have students practice reading it again. Model the correct voice intonation for reading a question. Then have students echo, trying to produce the same intonation.
- Distribute copies of page 62.
- Encourage students to practice reading lines from the poem with different ending punctuation marks.

Comprehension

- Discuss which animal is the predator and which animal is the prey in the poem.
- Ask students to brainstorm other pairs of animals that are predator and prey. Write students' responses on the board or on a sheet of chart paper.

Word Study Extension

Use page 63 to extend word concepts from the poem.

Mouse in the House

Oh, no! There's a mouse
Right here in the house.
He's here, right here,
Right here in the house!

He'd better scat—
Here comes the cat!
The cat, the cat!
He'd better scat!

—Karen McGuigan Brothers

Name:________________________

How Does It End?

Directions: Ending marks give clues about how to read sentences. Practice reading these lines from the poem in different ways.

.	Periods tell us the sentence is a statement. Practice reading these sentences as if you were telling your mom what you want for lunch.
Here comes the cat.	
He'd better scat.	

?	Question marks help us know a question is being asked. Practice reading these sentences as if you want to be sure of what you heard.
Here comes the cat?	
He'd better scat?	

!	Exclamation points show us excitement. Practice reading these sentences as if you are telling your mom what you want for your birthday.
Here comes the cat!	
He'd better scat!	

Name: ____________________

Word Building

I. Directions: Write words from the poem in the correct groups. Then add new words to each group.

Words with *-ouse*	Words with *-at*	Words About Mice

II. Directions: Read each sentence. Write the missing word. Use the Word Bank for help.

1. A barn is a ____________________ for cows.

2. My little brother can be a ____________________.

3. A ____________________ looks like a small rat.

4. Dad and I had a long ____________________.

Word Bank

chat   house   mouse   brat

Oh, Fall!

See pages 10–11 for ideas to introduce the poem. Complete some or all of the following activities throughout the week. The activities on this page may be completed before, during, or after reading the poem. Select activities based on your students' needs.

Phonemic Awareness

- Tell students that you are going to say a word and then ask them to change the beginning sound to make a new word. Say the word *fall*. Have students change the /f/ in *fall* to /b/. Students should respond with *ball*.
- Practice with the words listed below:

  Change the /h/ in *hall* to /k/—*call*

  Change the /k/ in *call* to /t/—*tall*

  Change the /t/ in *tall* to /w/—*wall*

  Change the /w/ in *wall* to /sm/—*small*

Phonics

- Distribute copies of page 66.
- Ask students to change the letter that makes the beginning sound to make a new word that matches the picture.

Vocabulary

- Tell students that another word for *fall* is *autumn*. These words are *synonyms*. Identify synonyms as words that have the same or nearly the same meaning.
- Have students recite the seasons of the year, using the word *autumn* in place of the word *fall*.
- Continue practicing with synonyms by asking the class to brainstorm synonyms for the word *beautiful* (e.g., *lovely*, *gorgeous*, *pretty*, *attractive*).

Fluency

- Use a pointer or a flashlight to point to the words as students read the poem. Tell students that they must keep pace with the pointer at all times.
- Move the pointer at an appropriate pace for your students. If you pause, so must they. If you speed up, they must as well.

Comprehension

- Ask students to name the seasons of the year. List the seasons in order on the board or on a sheet of chart paper. Relate the sequence of the seasons to the third line of the poem.
- Ask students to brainstorm things they associate with fall. Write students' responses on the board or on the sheet of chart paper.
- Ask students why the author of the poem thinks fall is "most beautiful of all." Have students provide other reasons why they like fall.

Word Study Extension

Use page 67 to extend word concepts from the poem.

Oh, Fall!

Oh, fall, oh, fall,
Oh, beautiful fall!
When colorful leaves
Start to fall,
Summer's over.
Winter will soon call.
Fall, oh, fall,
Most beautiful of all.

—Tim Rasinski

Name: ____________________

Make New Words

I. Directions: Change the letter that makes the beginning sound to make a new word. Write the new word on the line.

1. Change **fill** to  ____________________

2. Change **will** to  ____________________

3. Change **call** to  ____________________

4. Change **fall** to  ____________________

5. Change **hall** to 

____

II. Directions: Change the letter that makes the middle sound to make a new word. Write the new word on the line.

6. Change **ball** to  ____________________

7. Change **wall** to  ____________________

Name:________________________

Word Building

I. Directions: Write words from the poem in the correct groups. Then add new words to each group.

Words with *-all*	Words with *-ill*	Words About the Fall Season

II. Directions: Read each sentence. Write the missing word. Use the Word Bank for help.

1. Another name for autumn is ________________________.

2. In fall I can feel a ________________________ in the air.

3. My dog likes to chase ________________________.

4. Dad ________________________ the car with gas today.

Word Bank

chill fall filled balls

Blueberry Pancakes

See pages 10–11 for ideas to introduce the poem. Complete some or all of the following activities throughout the week. The activities on this page may be completed before, during, or after reading the poem. Select activities based on your students' needs.

Phonemic Awareness

- Tell students that you are going to say a word. They are to delete the first sound in the word to make a new word. Tell them to say *stack* without the /s/ sound. Students should respond with the word *tack*.
- Continue with the words below:

  Delete the /f/ in *fought—ought*

  Delete the /s/ in *stakes—takes*

  Delete the /f/ in *flake—lake*

Phonics

- Distribute copies of page 70.
- Ask students to sort the /ā/ vowel words and the /ă/ vowel words from the poem. Ask students to add two words of their own to each column. Once students have had time to complete the activity, have them compare their lists with partners.

Vocabulary

- Discuss the meaning of the word *stack* with students.
- Ask students what things can be stacked. Have students tell what they think a short stack and a tall stack of pancakes are. Have students draw a picture of each.
- Encourage students to look for a short stack and a tall stack of pancakes on the breakfast menu the next time they go out to eat.

Fluency

- Divide the class into two groups. Assign one group the first part of the poem. Assign the other group the second part of the poem.
- Ask the members of the first group to practice reading their part as if they are excited to eat a huge stack of pancakes. Ask the second group to practice reading their part as if they have a stomachache. Read the poem through several times using this grouping, and then have the groups switch roles.

Comprehension

- Ask students what they think the phrase *the cakes fought back* means. Ask students to use other lines from the poem to support their answers.
- Ask students to write about a time they had a stomachache. What kind of food did they eat? Did they eat too much?

Word Study Extension

Use page 71 to extend word concepts from the poem.

Blueberry Pancakes

Once, Jane and Jack
Tried to attack
A giant stack
of blueberry pancakes.

The cakes fought back
And Jane and Jack
Got an attack
Of blueberry tummy aches.

—Tim Rasinski

Name:________________________

Short or Long *A*?

Directions: Read each word in the Word Bank. Listen to the *a* vowel sound as you pronounce each word. Write each word in the correct column. Add two new words of your own to each column.

Word Bank

cakes	aches
Jane	back
stack	Jack

Short *A*—/ă/	Long *A*—/ā/

Name:____________________

Word Building

I. Directions: Write words from the poem in the correct groups. Then add new words to each group.

Words with *-ack*	Words with *-ake*	Words About Food

II. Directions: Read each sentence. Write the missing word. Use the Word Bank for help.

1. My birthday ____________________ has seven candles.
2. I ran around the ____________________ two times.
3. The water in the ____________________ is cold.
4. I have to ____________________ my backpack.

Word Bank

pack track cake lake

Babysitting Dogs

See pages 10–11 for ideas to introduce the poem. Complete some or all of the following activities throughout the week. The activities on this page may be completed before, during, or after reading the poem. Select activities based on your students' needs.

Phonemic Awareness

- Tell students that you are going to say a word, and then ask them to change the beginning sound to make a new word. Say the word *dog*. Have students change the /d/ in *dog* to /f/. Students should respond with *fog*.
- Practice with the words listed below:

  Change the /ŏ/ in *fog* to /ĭ/—*fig*

  Change the /f/ in *fig* to /p/—*pig*

  Change the /g/ in *pig* to /n/—*pin*

  Change the /ĭ/ in *pin* to /ĕ/—*pen*

Phonics

- Say the words *lazy* and *baby*. Ask students what sound they hear at the end of both words.
- Write the words on the board or on a sheet of chart paper. Have students identify the *y* as the letter that is making the /ē/ sound. Tell students that when a word ends in *y* and has another vowel in the word, the ending sound is usually /ē/.
- Ask students to use this knowledge to spell the following words:

bunny	*story*
sunny	*many*
smelly	*fairy*

Vocabulary

- Discuss the meaning of *synonyms* (words with the same or nearly the same meanings). Write the words *pooch, snoozes, yip,* and *sniffs* on the board or on a sheet of chart paper. Ask students to identify synonyms for each word. Record students' responses.
- Post the list in your room and regularly add new words as students think of them.

Fluency

- Select one synonym for each word from the vocabulary activity. Rewrite the poem using the synonyms in place of the words in the poem.
- Ask students which version they liked to read better and why.

Comprehension

- Distribute copies of page 74.
- Tell students to cut out the pictures and sentence strips at the bottom of the page. They should glue each card and picture in the correct column.

Word Study Extension

Use page 75 to extend word concepts from the poem.

Babysitting Dogs

One lazy pooch snoozes
Out under the sun,
While out in the field
Three more yip and run,
And another sniffs
At my hot dog bun.
Dogsitting, I think,
Can be lots of fun.

—*Tim Rasinski*

Name: ______________________

What Is Happening?

Directions: Cut out the picture cards and sentence strips at the bottom of the page. Glue the picture cards and sentence strips in the correct columns to illustrate and explain the lines from the poem.

One lazy pooch snoozes out under the sun.	While out in the field three more yip and run.	And another sniffs at my hot dog bun.

A dog is smelling my hot dog bun.	Dogs are barking and running in the field.	A lazy dog is taking a nap in the sun.

Name: ____________________

Word Building

I. Directions: Write words from the poem in the correct groups. Then add new words to each group.

Words with *-un*	Words with *-og*	Words About Dogs

II. Directions: Read each sentence. Write the missing word. Use the Word Bank for help.

1. My dad and I ______________ every day around our block.
2. The summer ______________ can give you a sunburn.
3. We burn ______________ in our fireplace.
4. Swimming in a pool is a lot of ______________.

Word Bank

sun jog fun logs

Birthday

See pages 10–11 for ideas to introduce the poem. Complete some or all of the following activities throughout the week. The activities on this page may be completed before, during, or after reading the poem. Select activities based on your students' needs.

Phonemic Awareness

- Tell students that you are going to say a word and then ask them to change the beginning sound to make a new word. Say the word *low*. Have students change the /l/ in *low* to /m/. Students should respond with *mow*.
- Practice with the words listed below:

  Change the /m/ in *mow* to /r/—*row*

  Change the /r/ in *row* to /sh/—*show*

  Change the /sh/ in *show* to /gl/—*glow*

Phonics

- Write the words *blow, show,* and *glow* on the board or on a sheet of chart paper. Ask students to identify the letters that are the same in all three words.
- Underline the letters *ow* in all three words. Tell students that the /ō/ sound at the end of a word often has the *ow* spelling pattern.
- Ask students to practice spelling the following words: *bow, low, row,* and *mow.*

Vocabulary

- Discuss the meaning of the word *glow*. How does this word describe a candle? Does the candle have to be lit in order for it to glow? Brainstorm other things that glow. Record student's responses.
- Ask each student to draw a picture and write a sentence about something that glows. Encourage students to use the word *glow* in their sentences.

Fluency

- Help students build fluency by encouraging them to pause in the correct places when reading the poem.
- Distribute copies of page 78.
- Tell students to take a short pause when they see one slash mark (/). Have them take a longer pause when they see two slash marks (//). After they have practiced reading the poem several times with the slash marks shown, encourage them to return to page 77 to read the poem without the slash marks.

Comprehension

- Ask students to identify things associated with birthdays and birthday cakes. Discuss the tradition of making a wish when blowing out the candles on the cake.
- Have students write about what they will wish for on their next birthday. Encourage students to draw a picture showing them blowing out the candles on the cake.

Word Study Extension

Use page 79 to extend word concepts from the poem.

Birthday

Candles on the cake,
See them glow.
Friends gathered 'round,
What a show!
Hold your breath still,
Not time to blow.
Sing "Happy Birthday,"
Nice and slow.
Make your wish...
Okay, now blow!

—Tim Rasinski

Name: ____________________

Pause Please

Directions: Practice reading "Birthday" with the phrasing shown below. Take a short pause when you see one slash mark (**/**). Take a longer pause when you see two slash marks (**//**).

Birthday

Candles on the cake, **/**
See them glow. **//**

Friends gathered 'round, **/**
What a show! **//**

Hold your breath still, **/**
Not time to blow. **//**

Sing "Happy Birthday," **/**
Nice and slow. **//**

Make your wish...**//**
Okay, now blow! **//**

—*Tim Rasinski*

Practice reading the poem again without looking at the slash marks.

Name: ____________________

Word Building

I. **Directions:** Write words from the poem in the correct groups. Then add new words to each group.

Words with *-ow*	Words with *-ake*	Words About Birthdays

II. **Directions:** Read each sentence. Write the missing word. Use the Word Bank for help.

1. Dad stepped on the ____________________ to stop.
2. Turtles tend to walk very ____________________.
3. I think ____________________ are creepy!
4. The lightbulb gave off a faint ____________________.

Word Bank

brakes glow snakes slowly

Pickles

See pages 10–11 for ideas to introduce the poem. Complete some or all of the following activities throughout the week. The activities on this page may be completed before, during, or after reading the poem. Select activities based on your students' needs.

Phonemic Awareness

- Read the phrase *tickle my tongue* from the poem. Brainstorm other parts of the body. Write students' responses on the board or on a sheet of chart paper.
- Ask students to think of an action word that begins with the same sound as each part of the body. For example, students could create the phrases *nuzzle my nose* or *flick my fingers*.

Phonics

- Encourage students to identify words in the poem that have smaller words within them. Help students identify and read the smaller words to help them read the larger words.
- Practice with the words from the poem listed below:

  dill—ill

  pickles—pick

  bread—read

  hamburger—ham and *burger*

  sandwich—sand, and, and *an*

Vocabulary

- Discuss the difference between *sweet pickles* and *dill pickles*. If possible, bring in samples of each for students to taste.
- Tell students that dill pickles are made with the dill herb. Brainstorm other herbs with which students may be familiar. Write students' responses on the board or on a sheet of chart paper.

Fluency

- Distribute copies of page 82.
- Ask students to look at the poem to find the words listed in the graph. Tell students to graph the number of times the words appear in the poem. Recognizing these words quickly will help students read the poem more fluently.

Comprehension

- Discuss with students the phrase *tickle my tongue*. Brainstorm other foods that may cause the tongue to tickle. Write students' responses on the board or on a sheet of chart paper.
- Ask students to name some foods that may cause another sensation on the tongue, such as foods that are slippery or foods that are hot.

Word Study Extension

Use page 83 to extend word concepts from the poem.

Pickles

Sweet pickles, dill pickles,
Tickle my tongue.
Eat them on bread
Or a hamburger bun.
A pickle sandwich
Is so much fun.
Sweet pickles, dill pickles,
Tickle my tongue.

—*Tim Rasinski*

Name: ____________________

Pickles Graph

Directions: Complete the graph below by shading the number of times each word appears in the poem "Pickles." Then answer the questions at the bottom of the page.

Poem Word	1	2	3	4	5	6
dill						
sweet						
or						
tongue						
pickles						
my						

1. Which word appears the most? ____________________

2. Which word appears the least? ____________________

3. Which word is your favorite word to say? ____________________

Name: ____________________

Word Building

I. Directions: Write words from the poem in the correct groups. Then add new words to each group.

Words with *-un*	Words with *-ick*	Words About Pickles

II. Directions: Read each sentence. Write the missing word. Use the Word Bank for help.

1. I am ____________________ for a hot dog.
2. The clowns put on a ____________________ act.
3. I stayed home today because I was ____________________.
4. A ____________________ hopped across our yard.

Word Bank

funny hungry bunny sick

The Rainbow

See pages 10–11 for ideas to introduce the poem. Complete some or all of the following activities throughout the week. The activities on this page may be completed before, during, or after reading the poem. Select activities based on your students' needs.

Phonemic Awareness

- Have students isolate the beginning sound in the words *shines* and *shades*. Ask students to brainstorm other words that have the /sh/ sound.
- Distribute copies of page 86.
- Ask students to sort the picture cards by words that begin with the /sh/ sound and words that end with the /sh/ sound.

Phonics

- Write the words *shines* and *shades* on the board or on a sheet of chart paper. Ask students to identify which letters make the /sh/ sound. Underline the letters *sh*.
- Ask students to practice spelling the following words: *shape, shake,* and *sharp*.

Vocabulary

- Discuss the term *shade*. Help students gain a better understanding of the word shade by having them make a shade card.
- Distribute 3" x 5" index cards to each student. Ask each student to select a crayon. Tell students to begin shading one side of the index card very lightly. As the students shade towards the other end of the index card, the shading should get darker and darker.
- Ask students to label the middle of their card with the name of the color. Tell students to write the word *light* on the side of the card that has light shading. Tell students to write the word *dark* on the side of the card that has dark shading.

Fluency

- Write the poem on the board or on a sheet of chart paper. Using colored markers, write the names of the colors in the poem. For example, use a green marker to write the word *green*.
- Ask students to practice reading the color words several times. Then have students read the poem in its entirety. Having each color word written in its own color will enable students to recognize the words more quickly, increasing fluency.

Comprehension

- Distribute watercolor paints to students. Ask each student to paint a rainbow.
- Tell students that they may use other colors; however, they should be sure to include the colors that are mentioned in the poem. Copy the poem and glue a copy of it in the corner or on the back of each painting.

Word Study Extension

Use page 87 to extend word concepts from the poem.

The Rainbow

When the sun shines after a rain,
The rainbow brightly comes again.
Shades of red and blue and green,
And orange and purple can be seen.

—Karen McGuigan Brothers

Name:__________________________

Shhhhh!

Directions: Cut out the picture cards at the bottom of the page. Say the name of each picture. Glue the picture cards in the correct column.

Begins like *shoes* 	**Ends like *brush*** 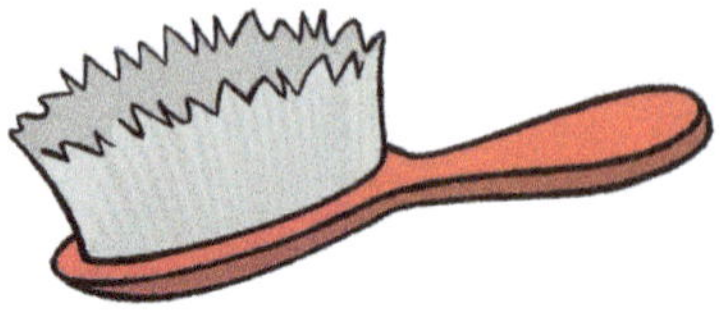

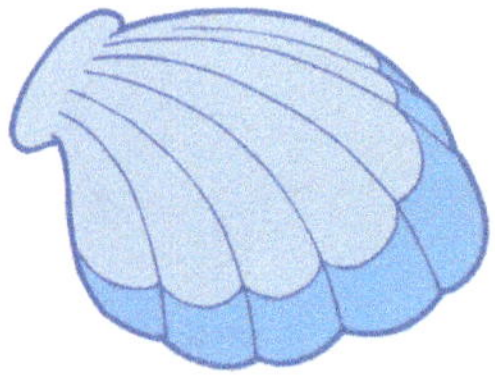

Name: ____________________

Word Building

I. Directions: Write words from the poem in the correct groups. Then add new words to each group.

Words with *-ain*	Words with *-een*	Words About Rainbows

II. Directions: Read each sentence. Write the missing word. Use the Word Bank for help.

1. Have you ____________________ my brother?
2. The dog was ____________________ to a pole.
3. My favorite colors are ____________________ and gold.
4. I like to stay dry on a ____________________ day.

Word Bank

rainy seen chained green

Castle

See pages 10–11 for ideas to introduce the poem. Complete some or all of the following activities throughout the week. The activities on this page may be completed before, during, or after reading the poem. Select activities based on your students' needs.

Phonemic Awareness

- Tell students that you will say some words. They are to identify the sound they hear at the end of each word. Ask students what sound they hear at the end of the word *castle*. Students should respond with the /l/ sound.
- Continue with the words listed below:

  beach—/ch/ sound

  today— /ā/ sound

  sand—/d/ sound

Phonics

- Ask students what sound they hear at the end of the word *beach*. Students should respond with the /ch/ sound. Tell students the letters *ch* make the /ch/ sound.
- Ask students to brainstorm other words that have the /ch/ sound. Write students' responses on the board or on a sheet of chart paper.
- Ask students to sort the words into two categories: words that begin with *ch* and words that end with *ch*.

Vocabulary

- Ask students to explain the meaning of the word *grand*. Encourage students to name other things that are grand.
- Have students draw a picture and write a sentence about something that is grand.

Fluency

- Read the first stanza of the poem to students. Ask students how they would feel after having built a sand castle. Have students practice reading the first stanza of the poem in a very proud voice.
- Read the first two lines of the second stanza of the poem. Ask students how they would feel if a wave washed it away. Have students read those lines in a sad voice.
- Read the last two lines of the second stanza to students. Ask students how they think the author of the poem feels at the end. Is she optimistic, realistic, or frustrated? Have students determine a voice tone in which to practice reading the last two lines of the poem.

Comprehension

- Distribute copies of page 90.
- Discuss the sequence of events in the poem. Ask students to glue the pictures in the correct sequence.

Word Study Extension

Use page 91 to extend word concepts from the poem.

Castle

I built a big castle.
It looked so very grand.
I built it on the beach.
I made it out of sand.

Suddenly a wave came
And washed it all away.
I'll build an even bigger one,
But maybe not today.

—Karen McGuigan Brothers

Name: ______________________

Sequence the Poem

Directions: Cut out the picture cards at the bottom of the page. Glue the cards in the correct sequence at the top of the page.

1	2	3
I built a big castle.	A wave came and washed it all away.	I'll build a bigger castle.

Name: ____________________

Word Building

I. Directions: Write words from the poem in the correct groups. Then add new words to each group.

Words with *-and*	Words with *-ay*	Words About Sand Castles

II. Directions: Read each sentence. Write the missing word. Use the Word Bank for help.

1. On Fridays, I can ____________________ up late.
2. My brother plays trumpet in the ____________________.
3. The statue is made of ____________________.
4. My favorite ____________________ is chocolate.

Word Bank

clay stay candy band

Sailboats

See pages 10–11 for ideas to introduce the poem. Complete some or all of the following activities throughout the week. The activities on this page may be completed before, during, or after reading the poem. Select activities based on your students' needs.

Phonemic Awareness

- Tell students that you are going to say a word. They are to delete the first sound in the word to make a new word. Tell students to say the word *boats* without the /b/ sound. Students should respond with *oats*.
- Continue with the words below:

  Delete the /h/ in *had—ad*

  Delete the /th/ in *that—at*

  Delete the /s/ in *slow—low*

Phonics

- Write the words *sail, boats, green,* and *sheets* on the board or on a sheet of chart paper. Ask students to identify the vowels in each word.
- Tell students that often when two vowels are together, the word usually has a long vowel sound. Read the following words and have students identify what vowel sound they hear:

  meat *pain* *queen* *laid*

Vocabulary

- Point to the phrase *snow-white sails* in the poem. Ask students to tell how having the word *snow* adds to the description of the white sails.
- Tell students that they will identify other words that describe colors by drawing pictures to match the color word.
- Distribute copies of page 94.

Fluency

- Increase color word recognition by having students rewrite the poem using other color words in place of *blue* and *green.* (The color word *red* must remain in place in order for the rhyme to still work.) For example, the line could be rewritten to read *pink or orange or red.*
- Tell students to practice reading their new poems to classmates.

Comprehension

- If possible, bring in several pictures of sailboats. Ask students to identify the setting in which they would most likely find sailboats.
- Discuss the importance of the sail in helping to move the sailboat across the water. Have each student draw a picture that illustrates the poem. The illustrations should be of a blue or green sailboat with a white sail.

Word Study Extension

Use page 95 to extend word concepts from the poem.

Sailboats

I love sailboats
Blue or green or red,
With snow-white sails
Like sheets on a bed.

—Karen McGuigan Brothers

Name: ____________________

Describing Color

Directions: Sometimes words are used to describe colors. Use a word from the Word Bank to describe the colors below. Write the word on the line. Then draw a picture of the selected word.

Word Bank

canary blood crow celery snow sky

1. ____________ **red**	2. ____________ **blue**
3. ____________ **white**	4. ____________ **green**
5. ____________ **black**	6. ____________ **yellow**

Name: ____________________

Word Building

I. **Directions:** Write words from the poem in the correct groups. Then add new words to each group.

Words with *-een*	Words with *-ail*	Words About Sailboats

II. **Directions:** Read each sentence. Write the missing word. Use the Word Bank for help.

1. Have you ____________________ my backpack?
2. My dog always wags his ____________________.
3. I ____________________ a letter to Grandma.
4. I am wearing a ____________________ shirt.

Word Bank

seen mailed tail green

Addition

See pages 10–11 for ideas to introduce the poem. Complete some or all of the following activities throughout the week. The activities on this page may be completed before, during, or after reading the poem. Select activities based on your students' needs.

Phonemic Awareness

- Tell students that you are going to say three words. They are to tell you which word does not begin with the same sound as the other two words.
- Say the words *two*, *twelve*, and *nine*. Students should respond with *nine* as the word that does not belong.
- Continue with the words listed below:

  four, one, five—one doesn't belong

  ten, three, thirty—ten doesn't belong

  eight, eighty, four—four doesn't belong

Phonics

- Tell students that the words *four* and *more* are the rhyming words in the poem. Write both words on the board or on a sheet of chart paper
- Discuss the two different spellings of the /or/ sound. Have students read the word *four* and then practice spelling the word *pour*. Have students read the word *more* and then practice spelling the following words: *bore, chore, core, score, store,* and *wore*.

Vocabulary

- Write the words *eight* and *ate* on the board or on a sheet of chart paper. Ask students to identify which of these words is in the poem.
- As a class, determine definitions for the words *eight* and *ate*.
- Write the sentences below on the board or on a sheet of chart paper. Have students identify whether the word *eight* or *ate* would make sense in each sentence.

  We ______ pancakes for breakfast. (*ate*)

  The dog had ______ puppies. (*eight*)

  My sister is ______ years old. (*eight*)

  He already ______ dinner. (*ate*)
- Have students create their own sentences to show the meaning of each word.

Fluency

- Distribute copies of page 98.
- Ask students to practice reading the poem several times as it is written with numbers. Tell students to cut out and glue the word cards in the correct order to rewrite the poem with number words.
- Pair students and have them practice reading the poem together.

Comprehension

- Relate the poem to math by having students rewrite the poem using number sentences. Ask why they think the author of the poem says, "I can't do any more."
- Encourage students to write other number sentences they can solve.

Word Study Extension

Use page 99 to extend word concepts from the poem.

Addition

One and one are two.
Two and two are four.
Four and four are eight.
I can't do any more.

—Karen McGuigan Brothers

Name:____________________

Number Words

Directions: Practice reading the poem several times as it is shown below. Then cut out the word cards at the bottom of the page. Glue the word cards in the correct boxes. Practice reading the poem with the number words.

1	and	1	are	2	.
2	and	2	are	4	.
4	and	4	are	8	.

I can't do any more.

One	Two	Four
one	two	four
two	four	eight

Name: ____________________

Word Building

I. Directions: Write words from the poem in the correct groups. Then add new words to each group.

Words with *-ore*	Words with *-and*	Words About Math

II. Directions: Read each sentence. Write the missing word. Use the Word Bank for help.

1. I built a ____________________ castle at the beach.

2. He ____________________ the sheet of paper.

3. She plays the drums in her ____________________.

4. The waves crashed against the ____________________.

Word Bank

shore tore band sand

The Toy Box

See pages 10–11 for ideas to introduce the poem. Complete some or all of the following activities throughout the week. The activities on this page may be completed before, during, or after reading the poem. Select activities based on your students' needs.

Phonemic Awareness

- Tell students that you are going to say a word. They are to say the word slowly, one sound at a time.
- Say the word *door*. Students should respond with /d/, /or/.
- Continue with the following words:

some—/s/, /ŭ/, /m/

and—/ă/, /n/, /d/

with—/w/, /ĭ/, /th/

Phonics

- Ask students to identify the beginning sound in the word *toy*. Students should respond with the /t/ sound.
- Create a list of words from the poem on the board or on a sheet of chart paper that begin with the letter *t*, end with the letter *t*, or have the letter *t* in the middle. Circle or underline the letter *t* in each word.
- Encourage students to think of other words that have the letter *t*. Add students' responses to the list.

Vocabulary

- Tell students that some of the toys in the toy box are old and some are new. Point out that the words *old* and *new* are opposites or *antonyms* of each other.
- Encourage students to think of other antonyms. Write students' responses on the board or on a sheet of chart paper.

Fluency

- Build fluency by rereading the poem.
- Read the poem to students in a normal voice. Then echo-read the poem by reading a line and having students read it back. Finally choral-read the poem together as a class.

Comprehension

- Distribute copies of page 102.
- Tell students to cut out the picture cards at the bottom of the page.
- After rereading the poem, have students glue the toys that are in the poem in the toy box. Read the poem again as a class to ensure that the students' pictures accurately show the toys from the poem.

Word Study Extension

Use page 103 to extend word concepts from the poem.

The Toy Box

Toys in the toy box,
Some old and some new.
Here's a puppet I got
When I was just two.
There's a teddy bear
From when I was four,
And a little car
With a moving door.

—Karen McGuigan Brothers

Name:______________________

Place It in the Toy Box

Directions: Cut out the picture cards at the bottom of the page. Glue pictures of toys mentioned in the poem in the toy box.

Challenge: Write the age when the toy was received next to the picture of the toy.

Name:____________________

Word Building

I. Directions: Write words from the poem in the correct groups. Then add new words to each group.

Words with -*ew*	Words with -*oy*	Words About Toys

II. Directions: Read each sentence. Write the missing word. Use the Word Bank for help.

1. I got a new __________________ for my birthday.
2. The bird __________________ to its nest.
3. Did you __________________ the show?
4. My dog likes to __________________ his bone.

Word Bank

flew chew toy enjoy

Peek-a-boo

See pages 10–11 for ideas to introduce the poem. Complete some or all of the following activities throughout the week. The activities on this page may be completed before, during, or after reading the poem. Select activities based on your students' needs.

Phonemic Awareness

- Ask students to identify the ending sound in the word *me*. Students should respond with the /ē/ sound.
- Ask students to brainstorm other words that also end with the /ē/ sound. Write students' responses on the board or on a sheet of chart paper.
- Distribute copies of page 106.
- Ask students to color the pictures that end with the same sound as the word *me*.

Phonics

- Write the words *peek* and *tree* on the board or on a sheet of chart paper. Ask students to identify the letters that make the /ē/ sound. Underline the *ee* spelling pattern.
- Ask students to practice writing the following words with the *ee* spelling pattern: *bee, meet, queen, jeep, sleep,* and *seed.*

Vocabulary

- Ask students to stand behind their desks. Once everyone is in position, tell students, "You are standing behind your desks."
- Give students other directions for them to practice modeling the word *behind*. If possible, take students outside and have them model hiding behind a tree.

Fluency

- Place a star at the beginning of the lines *What are you going to do?* in the poem. Model for students how to read this sentence.
- Encourage students to try to emulate the intonation of your voice as you read the question. Repeat the question several times, having the students echo you each time. Then practice reading the poem together. Encourage students to look ahead as they read the poem in order to be ready to read the question.

Comprehension

- Ask students with whom they might play the game of peek-a-boo. Have a pair of students demonstrate how to play peek-a-boo.
- Ask students to brainstorm possible places they could hide if they were playing peek-a-boo. Write students' responses on the board or on a sheet of chart paper.

Word Study Extension

Use page 107 to extend word concepts from the poem.

Peek-a-boo

Peek-a-boo,
I see you.
What are you
Going to do?
Peek-a-boo,
You see me,
Hiding there
Behind the tree.

—Karen McGuigan Brothers

Name:________________________

Ends Like Me

Directions: Say the name of each picture. Color the picture if it ends with the same sound as the word *me*.

1.

2.

3.

4.

5.
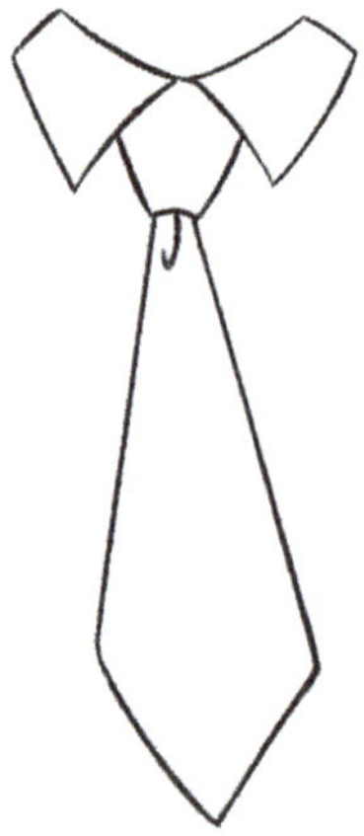

6.

7.

8.
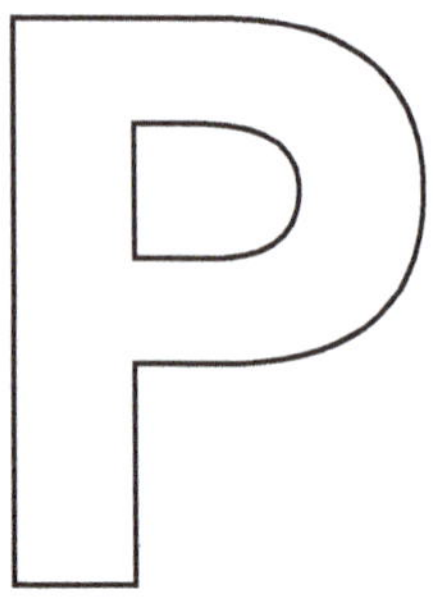

9.

Name: ______________________

Word Building

I. Directions: Write words from the poem in the correct groups. Then add new words to each group.

Words with -ee	Words with *-ing*	Words About Hiding

II. Directions: Read each sentence. Write the missing word. Use the Word Bank for help.

1. She is ______________________ from me.

2. My sister is ______________________ years old.

3. Cats are good at climbing ______________________.

4. We are ______________________ to Grandma's house.

Word Bank

hiding trees three going

I'll Fly a Plane

See pages 10–11 for ideas to introduce the poem. Complete some or all of the following activities throughout the week. The activities on this page may be completed before, during, or after reading the poem. Select activities based on your students' needs.

Phonemic Awareness

- Tell students that you are going to say a sound and a word. Ask them to tell you the new word that is made when you add the sound to the beginning of the word. Tell students to add the /p/ sound to the word *lane*. Students should respond with *plane*.
- Continue with the words below:

  Add /s/ to *pain—Spain*

  Add /g/ to *row—grow*

  Add /s/ to *take—stake*

Phonics

- Write the words *to* and *too* on the board or on a sheet of chart paper. Tell students that although these words sound the same, they are spelled differently and have different meanings.
- Locate the words *to* and *too* in the poem. Discuss the spelling and meaning of each word.
- Ask students to practice reading the following words with a similar ending sound: *do, boo, shoo, goo,* and *moo*.

Vocabulary

- Distribute copies of page 110.
- Ask students to color the countries shown on the map according to the key at the top of the page. Ask students to identify which countries are in the poem. Then ask which countries are not in the poem.

Fluency

- Read the poem together. Then divide the students into two groups.
- Assign one group to read the beginning part of the poem. Assign the other group to read the ending part of the poem. Read the poem several times and then have the groups switch roles.

Comprehension

- Ask students to think of something they want to be when they grow up. Tell them to write what they would be able to see or do in that profession.
- Compare students' ideas to the poem. Identify what the child in the poem wants to do when he or she grows up. What will that child be able to see or do?

Word Study Extension

Use page 111 to extend word concepts from the poem.

I'll Fly a Plane

When I grow up,
I'll fly a plane
To France or China
Or maybe Spain.

I'll fly so high,
Too high to see,
And take you up
Along with me.

—Karen McGuigan Brothers

Name: ______________________

Where in the World?

Directions: Look at this map of the world. Use the key to color the countries.

France = blue	China = yellow	Spain = red
United States = orange	Australia = green	Brazil = purple

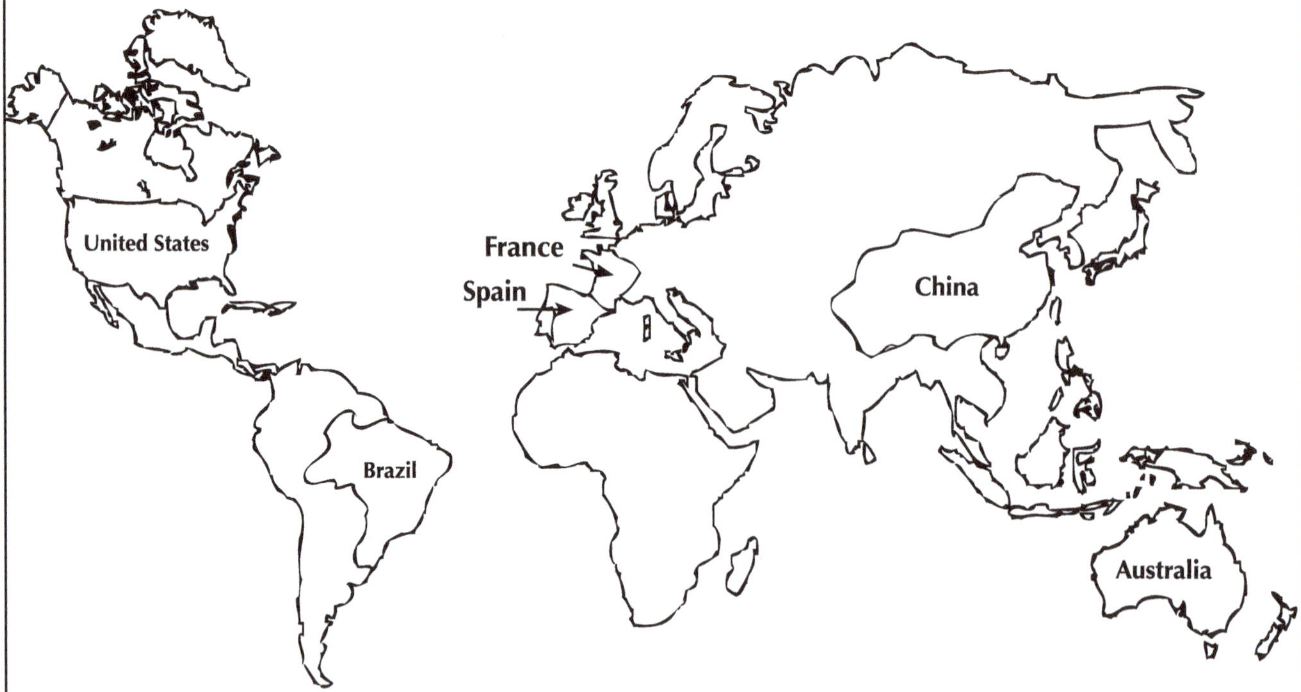

What is the name of the country where you live?

____

Name:________________________

Word Building

I. Directions: Write words from the poem in the correct groups. Then add new words to each group.

Words with *-ane*	Words with *-y*	Words About Flying

II. Directions: Read each sentence. Write the missing word. Use the Word Bank for help.

1. My grandpa uses a ____________________ to walk.
2. I love how the ____________________ is so blue today.
3. ____________________ mother reads to me every day.
4. A ____________________ is a beautiful bird.

Word Bank

crane sky cane My

The Bully

See pages 10–11 for ideas to introduce the poem. Complete some or all of the following activities throughout the week. The activities on this page may be completed before, during, or after reading the poem. Select activities based on your students' needs.

Phonemic Awareness

- Ask students what sound they hear at the end of the word *bully*. Students should respond with the /ē/ sound.
- Tell students that you are going to say some words. If a word has the same ending sound as *bully*, they are to show a thumbs-up sign. If a word has a different ending sound, they are to show a thumbs-down sign.

  Jimmy—thumbs-up sign

  puppy—thumbs-up sign

  fly—thumbs-down sign

  smelly—thumbs-up sign

Phonics

- Tell students that often the /ite/ sound is spelled *-ight*. Tell students to use their poem to find words with this spelling pattern.
- Ask students if they know another spelling pattern that makes the /ī/ sound. Students should identify CVCV (consonant-vowel-consonant-vowel) words with the /ī/ sound as the medial vowel and a silent *e* as the ending vowel.
- Distribute copies of page 114.
- Ask students to read the words on each kite. If the words are /ī/ words that rhyme, they should color the kite.

Vocabulary

- Discuss the word *bully*. Ask students what they think makes a bully.
- As a class, "quarter" the word *bully*. To do this, fold a sheet of chart paper into four sections or draw a rectangle on the board or on a sheet of chart paper. Divide the paper or the rectangle into four sections by drawing lines. In the first section, write the vocabulary word. In the second section, write a definition of the word. The third section should contain a picture of the word. The final section should include a sentence using the word.

Fluency

- Divide students into two groups. Have one group read the first part of the poem in the toughest voices possible. Have the second group of students read the second part of the poem in a gentle tone.
- Practice reading the poem several times and then have the groups switch roles.

Comprehension

- Discuss the last sentence of the poem.
- Have each student write a letter to Jimmy about why being a bully isn't right and why it's better to be nice.

Word Study Extension

Use page 115 to extend word concepts from the poem.

The Bully

My friend Jimmy
Likes to fight,
But I tell him
It isn't right.
If you're a bully,
Before you're through,
Someone bigger
Will bully you.

—*Karen McGuigan Brothers*

Name: ____________________________

Spelling Long *I*

Directions: Color each kite that has rhyming long *i* words.

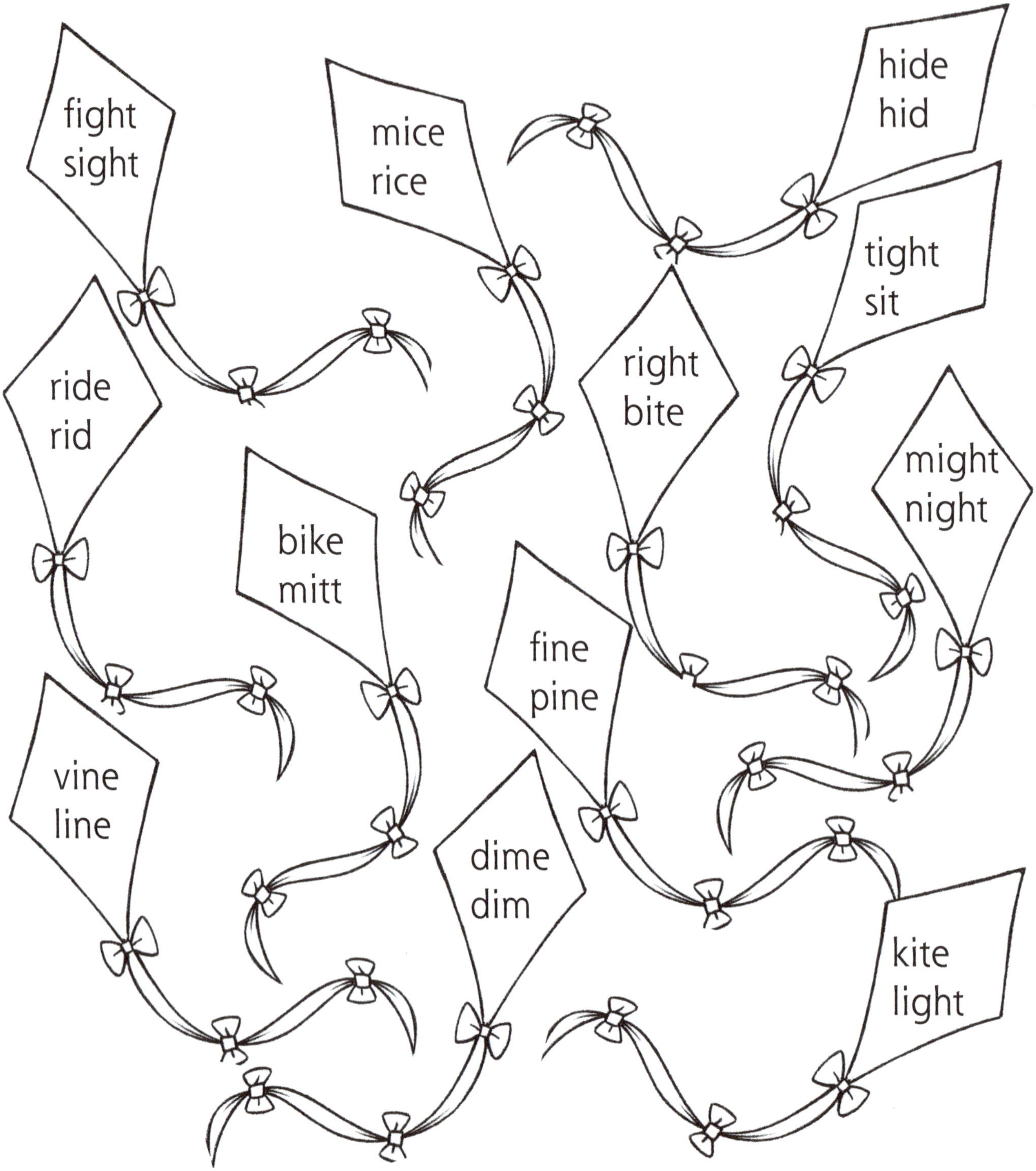

Name: ______________________

Word Building

I. Directions: Write words from the poem in the correct groups. Then add new words to each group.

Words with *-ight*	Words with *-im*	Words About Bullies

II. Directions: Read each sentence. Write the missing word. Use the Word Bank for help.

1. My brother and I ______________________ all the time.
2. The cup was chipped on its ______________________.
3. After I eat, my pants feel a bit ______________________ .
4. My mom ______________ my hair when it gets too long.

Word Bank

trims rim fight tight

Pancakes

See pages 10–11 for ideas to introduce the poem. Complete some or all of the following activities throughout the week. The activities on this page may be completed before, during, or after reading the poem. Select activities based on your students' needs.

Phonemic Awareness

- Tell students that you are going to say three words in succession and they need to identify the sound that is the same in all three words. Say the words *pancake*, *plate*, and *pound*. Students should respond that all three words have the same beginning /p/ sound.
- Continue with the list below:

  more, four, car—ending /r/ sound

  melt, more, munch—beginning /m/ sound

  wait, want, we—beginning /w/ sound

Phonics

- Discuss *compound words* with students. Tell them that a compound word is two words put together to make one word.
- Demonstrate how to separate a compound word into two individual words. For example, say the word *starfish*. Tell students that the word *starfish* can be separated into the two words *star* and *fish*. Discuss how this may be useful when trying to decode an unknown word.
- Distribute copies of page 118.

Vocabulary

- Discuss the term *melted* with students. Ask them to identify different ways things can be melted.
- Ask students to brainstorm different things that can melt. Ask students how they think the butter melts in the poem.

Fluency

- Demonstrate the effects of periods and exclamation points when reading sentences. Write a declarative sentence from the poem on the board or on a sheet of chart paper. Model the appropriate intonation for reading the sentence. Then have students emulate your intonation.
- Write a sentence from the poem that ends with an exclamation point on the board or on a sheet of chart paper. This time, model the appropriate intonation for reading a sentence with an exclamation point. Have students echo you, trying to produce the same intonation.
- Ask students to reread the poem and change their voice intonation to match the ending marks shown in the poem.

Comprehension

- Ask students to name their favorite food to eat for breakfast. Create a graph showing the favorite foods of the students in the class.
- Discuss which food is liked the most by students. Which food is liked least by the students?

Word Study Extension

Use page 119 to extend word concepts from the poem.

Pancakes

Pancakes for breakfast—
I can hardly wait!
With lots of melted butter
And syrup on my plate.

Pancakes for breakfast—
Give me three or four.
And when I've eaten them,
I think I'll have some more!

—Karen McGuigan Brothers

Name: ____________________

Compound Words

Directions: Say the name of each picture. Write the name of the picture on the line below. Create a compound word by combining the two words. Use the Word Bank to help you.

1.  + 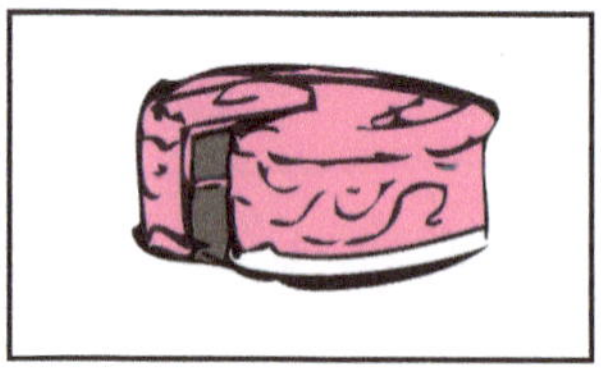 = 

____________ ____________ ____________

2.  +  = 

____________ ____________ ____________

3. 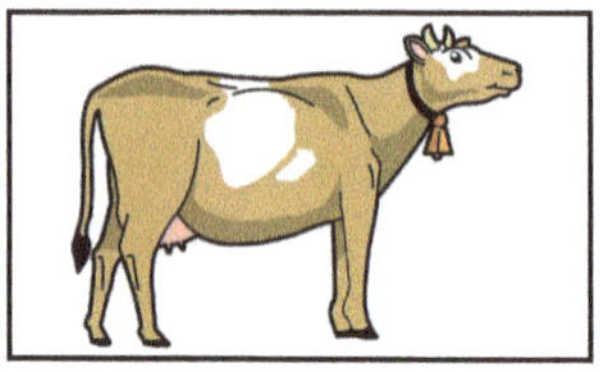 +  = 

____________ ____________ ____________

4.  +  = 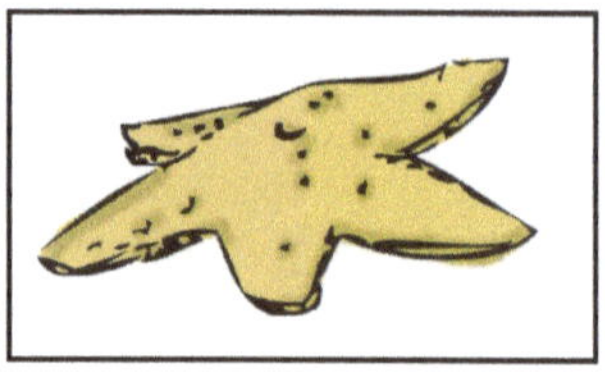

____________ ____________ ____________

Word Bank

cake rain boy fish bow star pan cow

Name: ____________________

Word Building

I. Directions: Write words from the poem in the correct groups. Then add new words to each group.

Words with *-ast*	Words with *-ate*	Words About Pancakes

II. Directions: Read each sentence. Write the missing word. Use the Word Bank for help.

1. My dad always says, "Don't be ______________ for school."
2. Jimmy can run really ______________.
3. California is a ______________.
4. The doctor took the ______________ off my arm today.

Word Bank

late state fast cast

Pancakes

See pages 10–11 for ideas to introduce the poem. Complete some or all of the following activities throughout the week. The activities on this page may be completed before, during, or after reading the poem. Select activities based on your students' needs.

Phonemic Awareness

- Tell students you are going to say a word and then ask them to change the beginning sound to make a new word. Say the word *mug*. Have students change the /m/ sound in *mug* to the /r/ sound. Students should respond with *rug*.
- Distribute copies of page 122.
- Ask students to find other words in the poem for which the beginning sound can be changed to create words that rhyme with *rug*. Students should write each word in a finger of the hand on the page.

Phonics

- Segment the word *bug* (/b/, /ŭ/, /g/). Point out the /ŭ/ sound.
- Ask students to brainstorm other words from the poem that have the /ŭ/ sound.
- Ask students to practice spelling these words: *cut, bus, sun, drum,* and *tub*.

Vocabulary

- Demonstrate for students how to shrug your shoulders. Have students do the same. Tell them that a shrug is a form of body language.
- Ask students what someone is "telling you" when they shrug their shoulders. Have students brainstorm other types of body language that can be shown with gestures.

Fluency

- Use a pointer or a flashlight to point to the words as students read the poem. Tell students that they must keep pace with the pointer at all times.
- Move the pointer at an appropriate pace for your students. If you pause, so must they. If you speed up, they must as well. Your students will find it amusing if you slow down or speed up considerably during this activity.

Comprehension

- Make the poem into a book by typing each line or phrase on its own page. Staple or bind the pages together in the correct order.
- Distribute copies of the book to each student and let him or her illustrate the book. You may also wish to have groups of students work on pages together to make a class book that everyone can read.

Word Study Extension

Use page 123 to extend word concepts from the poem.

Snug in a Rug

A boy, a bear, and a bug
Rolled themselves up inside a rug.
The boy gave a little tug,
The bear moved over and made a shrug,
But the little bitty bug
Was snug, snug, snug inside that rug!

—Tim Rasinski

Name: ____________________

A Handful of Rhymes

Directions: Change the beginning sound in the word *rug* to create four words from the poem that rhyme with rug. Then think of one more word. Write each word in a finger of the hand.

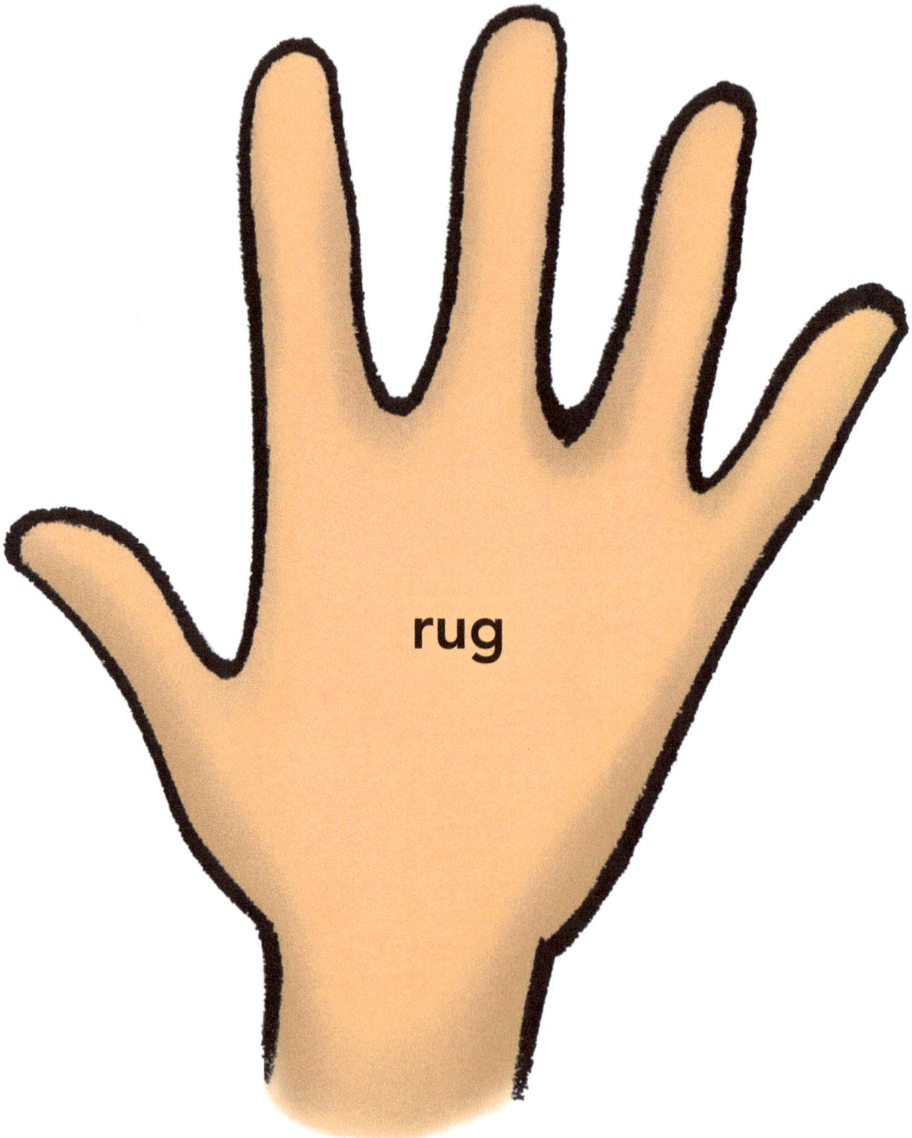

1. Which words name objects? ____________________

2. Which words name actions? ____________________

Name: ______________________

Word Building

I. Directions: Write words from the poem in the correct groups. Then add new words to each group.

Words with -*ug*	**Words with -*ade***	**Words About Bears**

II. Directions: Read each sentence. Write the missing word. Use the Word Bank for help.

1. I like to ______________________ up in my blanket.

2. The sun was so hot that we went into the ______________.

3. Dad's joke ______________________ me laugh.

4. The ______________________ was filled with water.

Word Bank

made snuggle shade jug

The Chair

See pages 10–11 for ideas to introduce the poem. Complete some or all of the following activities throughout the week. The activities on this page may be completed before, during, or after reading the poem. Select activities based on your students' needs.

Phonemic Awareness

- Tell students that you are going to say three words in succession and they need to identify the sound that is the same in all three words.
- Say the words *bug*, *boy*, and *bear*. Students should respond that all three words have the same beginning /b/ sound. Ask students to brainstorm other words that also begin with the /b/ sound. Write students' responses on the board or on a sheet of chart paper.
- Distribute copies of page 126.
- Tell students that they are to circle the word *yes* if the name of the picture begins with the /b/ sound. Students should circle *no* if the name of the picture begins with a different sound.

Phonics

- Have students write the word *bug* on a sheet of paper. Tell them to listen carefully to change each word to a new one.
- Read the script below. Have students spell a new word by changing one letter of the previous word.

  Change *bug* to *hug*.

  Change *hug* to *hut*.

  Change *hut* to *hat*.

  Change *hat* to *bat*.

  Change *bat* to *bet*.

Vocabulary

- Write the phrase *but the chair was too small* on the board or on a sheet of chart paper. Ask students what the phrase means.
- Ask students to brainstorm other instances of something being *too small*. Tell students to work in pairs to draw a picture of what *too small* means in this poem.

Fluency

- Divide students into groups of three or four. Ask students in each group to create actions to go along with the poem.
- Ask students to practice reading the poem several times while doing the actions. Then allow each group to perform the poem for the rest of the class, as they act it out.

Comprehension

- Have students make comparisons of the poem with the story *Goldilocks and the Three Bears*.
- Create a Venn diagram to show the similarities and differences between the poem and the story.

Word Study Extension

Use page 127 to extend word concepts from the poem.

The Chair

A bug, a boy, and a bear
Sat together in one small chair.
But the chair was too small
To fit them all.
That bug, that boy, and that bear.

—*Tim Rasinski*

Name:________________________

Begins the Same

Directions: Say the name of each picture. Circle the word *yes* if it begins with the same sound as *bug*, *boy*, and *bear*. Circle the word *no* if it does not begin with the same sound.

1. 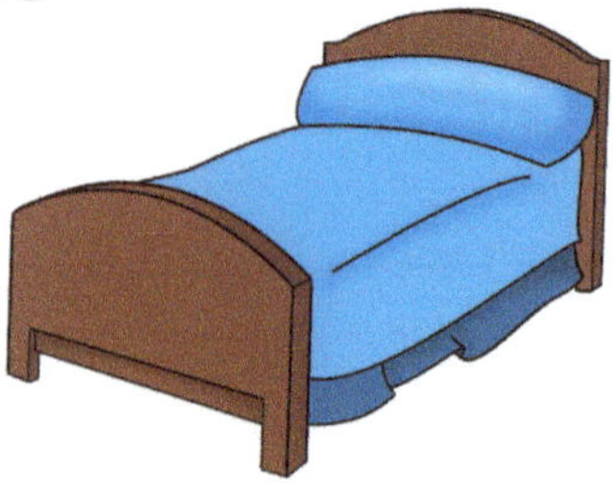 yes no	**2.** 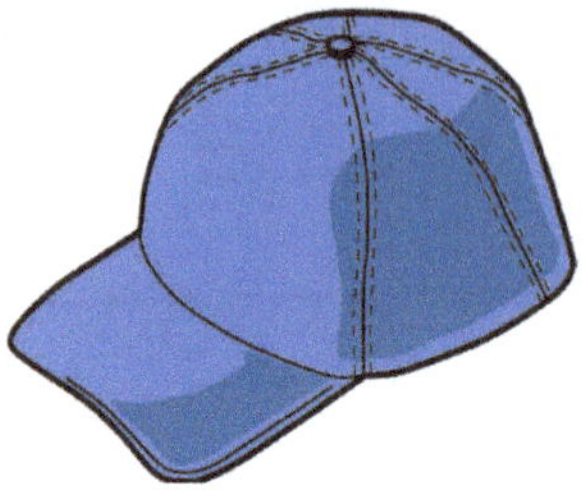 yes no	**3.**  yes no
4. 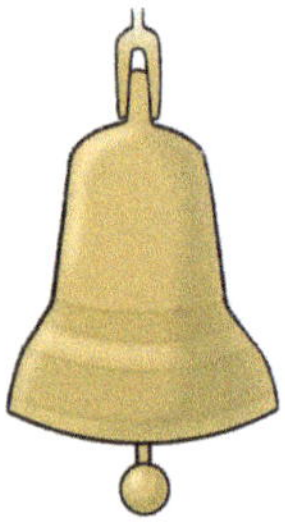 yes no	**5.**  yes no	**6.** 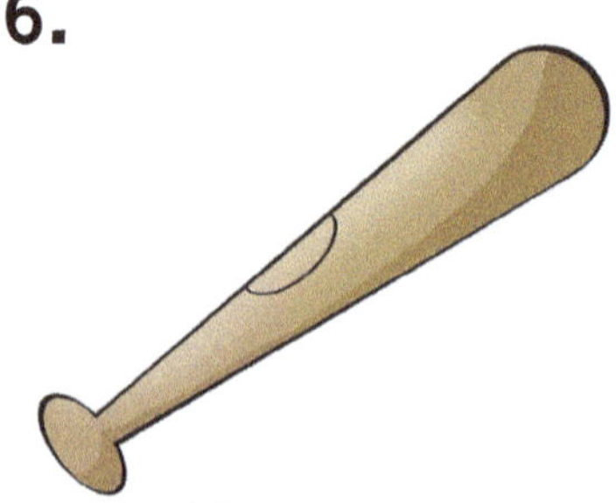 yes no
7.  yes no	**8.**  yes no	**9.**  yes no

Name: ______________________

Word Building

I. Directions: Write words from the poem in the correct groups. Then add new words to each group.

Words with *-air*	Words with *-all*	Words About Chairs

II. Directions: Read each sentence. Write the missing word. Use the Word Bank for help.

1. Dad likes to sit in a big fat ______________________.

2. My mother ______________________ me to come home.

3. I walked up the ______________________ to my bedroom.

4. My dad is ______________________ than my mom.

Word Bank

stairs chair called taller

Jump for Joy

See pages 10–11 for ideas to introduce the poem. Complete some or all of the following activities throughout the week. The activities on this page may be completed before, during, or after reading the poem. Select activities based on your students' needs.

Phonemic Awareness

- Tell students you are going to say three words. Two of the words will begin with the same sound. The other word will begin with a different sound. Students are to identify the word that does not belong. Say the words *bear*, *bug*, and *spot*. Students should respond that *spot* does not belong.
- Continue with the words listed below:

  boy, play, pig—boy doesn't belong

  jump, great, joy—great doesn't belong

  love, live, drive—drive doesn't belong

Phonics

- Ask students to identify the verbs in the poem. Underline the *-ed* at the end of each verb that makes it past tense. Discuss the sounds that *-ed* can make at the end of a word (/t/, /d/, or /ed/).
- Distribute copies of page 130.

Vocabulary

- Discuss with students the definition of the word *joy*. Create an acrostic poem by writing the word *joy* vertically. Ask students to think of a word or sentence that tells about something related to the word *joy* that begins with each letter of the word. For example:

  Jumping on a trampoline.

  Our mom bringing us a treat.

  You coming over to play with me.

Fluency

- Display the poem to students. Reread the poem several times as you play "Spotlight."
- Turn off the lights in the room and give a student a flashlight. Have him or her turn on the flashlight and use the light as a pointer. The rest of the students in the class should practice reading the poem, as the student with the flashlight tracks the words. Select other students to use the spotlight and reread the poem.

Comprehension

- Ask students what they like to play with their friends. What do they think a bear, a bug, and a boy would play?
- Ask each student to draw a picture and write about what would make the bear, bug, and boy "jump for joy" as they are playing.

Word Study Extension

Use page 131 to extend word concepts from the poem.

Jump for Joy

A bear, a bug, and a boy
Played and jumped for joy.
They loved to play,
And they played all day.
That bear, that bug, and that boy.

—*Tim Rasinski*

Name: ______________________

Add -*ed*

Directions: Add -*ed* to each word below to make it past tense. Circle the ending sound of the new word.

Word	Past Tense	Ending Sound
1. play		t d ed
2. jump		t d ed
3. follow		t d ed
4. mail		t d ed
5. brush		t d ed
6. fold		t d ed
7. crawl		t d ed
8. help		t d ed

Name: ____________________

Word Building

I. Directions: Write words from the poem in the correct groups. Then add new words to each group.

Words with *-ump*	Words with *-ay*	Words About Playtime

II. Directions: Read each sentence. Write the missing word. Use the Word Bank for help.

1. April is the month before ____________________.
2. I ____________________ air into my bike's tires.
3. Mom gave me lunch on a ____________________.
4. We ____________________ for joy when we won.

Word Bank

pumped jumped May tray

Oh, Summer!

See pages 10–11 for ideas to introduce the poem. Complete some or all of the following activities throughout the week. The activities on this page may be completed before, during, or after reading the poem. Select activities based on your students' needs.

Phonemic Awareness

- Tell students you are going to say a word from the poem. Students are to segment the word by saying the sounds they hear in the word, one sound at a time. Say the word vacation. Students should respond /v/, /ā/, /c/, /ā/, /sh/, /ŭ/, /n/.
- Continue with the following words:

  season—/s/, /ē/, /z/, /ə/, /n/

  school—/s/, /k/, /o͞o/, /l/

Phonics

- Write the words *summer* and *bummer* on the board or on a sheet of chart paper. Ask students to segment each word by saying one sound at a time.
- Ask students to identify the letters that make the /er/ sound at the end of each word. Tell students that the /er/ sound at the end of a word is often spelled *-er*.
- Practice reading or spelling the following words: *flower, her, baker, thunder,* and *powder*.

Vocabulary

- Discuss the meaning of the word *tramping* with students.
- Ask students to demonstrate what it means to tramp. Have students read the poem while tramping around the room.

Fluency

- Use a pointer or a flashlight to point to the words as students read the poem. Tell students that they must keep pace with the pointer at all times.
- Move the pointer at an appropriate pace for your students. If you pause, so must they. If you speed up, they must as well.

Comprehension

- Distribute copies of page 134.
- Ask students to brainstorm activities they like to do in the summer. Write students' responses on the board or on a sheet of chart paper.
- Ask students to name some summer activities from the poem. Compare and contrast the activities students like to do with those named in the poem.

Word Study Extension

Use page 135 to extend word concepts from the poem.

Oh, Summer!

Oh, summer, dear! Oh, summer, dear!
We're so glad that you are here.
You're a season of fun at the pool.

We'll be tramping and hiking.
We'll go camping and biking,
Until it is time to start school.

—Tim Rasinski

Name: ____________________

Summer Fun

I. Directions: Brainstorm activities you like to do in the summer.

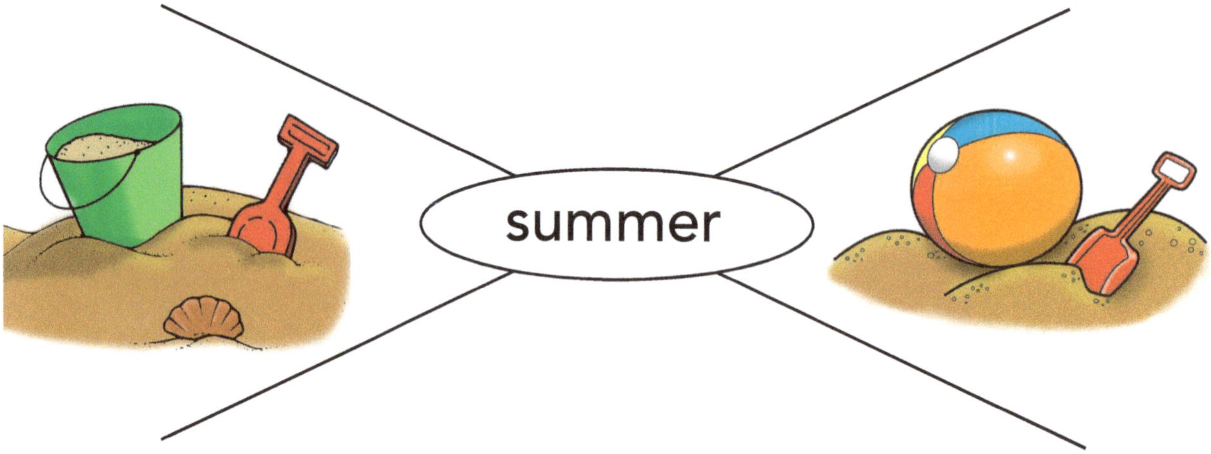

II. Directions: Name the summer activities from the poem.

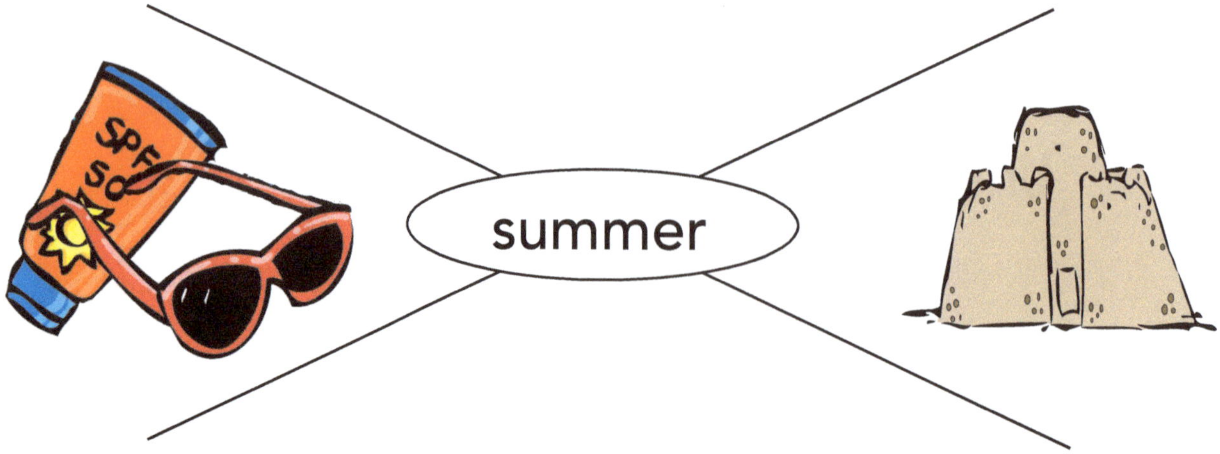

1. Did you think of any of the same activities as those in the poem?
   yes   no

2. What is your favorite summer activity? ____________________

____

Name: ____________________

Word Building

I. Directions: Write words from the poem in the correct groups. Then add new words to each group.

Words with *-amp*	Words with *-um*	Words About Summer Fun

II. Directions: Read each sentence. Write the missing word. Use the Word Bank for help.

1. The ____________________ of two and two is four.
2. I like to ____________________ in the woods.
3. The rain made our tent ____________________.
4. The mother ____________________ a song to her baby.

Word Bank

camp damp hummed sum

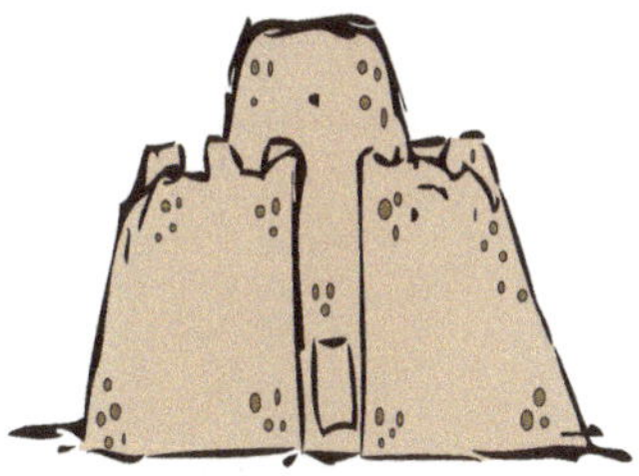

Page 18

1. beginning sound
2. beginning sound
3. beginning sound
4. ending sound
5. beginning sound
6. beginning sound
7. ending sound
8. ending sound
9. beginning sound

Page 19

Students' answers may vary. Sample answers are provided below.

Words with *-ool*

school pool
cool tool

Words with *-ook*

book took
hook look

Words About Summer Fun

beach swim
play tan

1. books
2. pool
3. look
4. school

Page 22

1. hat
2. jacket
3. shirt
4. jeans
5. belt
6. shoes

Students' answers for the two additional clothing items will vary. Examples: socks, skirt, mittens

Page 23

Students' answers may vary. Sample answers are provided below.

Words with *-ool*

cool school
tool fool

Words with *-ot*

got not
hot dot

Words About the First Day of School

exciting new
fun teacher

1. tot
2. cool
3. pool
4. lot

Page 26

Vegetable—carrot, potato, corn, peas

Not a Vegetable—cheese, apple, milk, egg

Page 27

Students' answers may vary. Sample answers are provided below.

Words with *-and*

and band
land stand

Words with *-ast*

fast last
cast past

Words About Gardens

vegetables dirt
weeds water

1. cast
2. band
3. last
4. sand

Page 30

1. The roller coaster goes up the track.
2. I look all around.
3. The roller coaster gets to the top.
4. The roller coaster goes down the track.

Page 31

Students' answers may vary. Sample answers are provided below.

Words with *-ack*

track back
tack pack

Words with *-op*

top drop
stop hop

Words About Roller Coasters

track ride
fast fun

1. Jack
2. stopped
3. pack
4. shop

Page 34

Students' answers should represent the appropriate sight and color words.

Page 35
Students' answers may vary. Sample answers are provided below.

Words with *-ick*

stick pick
lick quick

Words with *-eat*

treat seat eat
meat beat

Words About Treats

yummy sweet
special exciting

1. slick
2. beat
3. sick
4. meat

Page 38
1. bow
2. mow
3. row
4. tow
5. blow

Page 39
Students' answers may vary. Sample answers are provided below.

Words with *-ow*

glow know
low slow

Words with *-ark*

dark mark
bark park

Words About the Night

dark moon
stars owls

1. bark
2. glow
3. Mark
4. show

Page 42
1. wild
2. tame
3. tame
4. wild
5. wild
6. tame
7. tame
8. wild

Page 43
Students' answers may vary. Sample answers are provided below.

Words with *-ame*

tame same
came name
shame

Words with *-ild*

wild mild
child

Words About Animals

furry pets
friends smelly

1. Wild
2. came
3. same
4. child

Page 46
1. commotion
2. motion
3. notion
4. commotion
5. notion
6. motion

Page 47
Students' answers may vary. Sample answers are provided below.

Words with *-otion*

notion lotion
motion commotion

Words with *-ent*

invent dent
sent lent

Words About Being Smart

ideas brain
work brilliant

1. potion
2. went
3. motion
4. tent

Page 50
Students' answers may vary.

Page 51
Students' answers may vary. Sample answers are provided below.

Words with *-ame*

game same
tame frame

Words with *-y*

my fly
cry shy

Words About Games

television controllers
challenging fun

1. My
2. tame
3. try
4. same

Page 54

1. ends with /ick/
2. does not end with /ick/
3. ends with /ick/
4. ends with /ick/
5. does not end with /ick/
6. ends with /ick/
7. ends with /ick/
8. does not end with /ick/
9. does not end with /ick/

Page 55

Students' answers may vary. Sample answers are provided below.

Words with -ick

stick lick
pick sick

Words with -eat

treat eat
seat neat

Words About Treats

sweets yummy
snacks special

1. lick
2. heat
3. pick
4. meats

Page 58

Students' should be able to sing the poem to the tune of "Twinkle, Twinkle Little Star."

Page 59

Students' answers may vary. Sample answers are provided below.

Words with *-all*

tall ball
wall all

Words with *-ort*

short port
sort sport

Words About You

tall cute
fun friendly

1. sport
2. mall
3. short
4. stall

Page 62

Students should correctly read the poem lines from the poem based on the ending punctuation marks.

Page 63

Students' answers may vary. Sample answers are provided below.

Words with *-ouse*

mouse house
louse

Words with *-at*

cat scat
rat bat

Words About Mice

tails furry
small fast

1. house
2. brat
3. mouse
4. chat

Page 66

1. hill
2. mill
3. ball
4. wall
5. mall
6. bell
7. well

Page 67

Students' answers may vary. Sample answers are provided below.

Words with *-all*

fall call
all wall

Words with *-ill*

bill will
spill fill

Words About the Fall Season

colorful crunchy
cool beautiful

1. fall
2. chill
3. balls
4. filled

Page 70

Short *a*—Jack, stack, back
Long *a*—Jane, aches, cakes

Page 71

Students' answers may vary. Sample answers are provided below.

Words with *-ack*

Jack stack
attack back

Words with *-ake*

cake take
lake shake

Words About Food

yummy dinner
hungry spaghetti

1. cake
2. track
3. lake
4. pack

Page 74

One lazy pooch snoozes out under the sun.	While out in the field three more yip and run.	And another sniffs at my hot dog bun.
	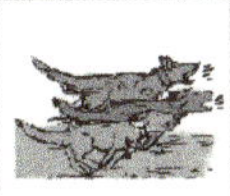	
A lazy dog is taking a nap in the sun.	Dogs are barking and running in the field.	A dog is smelling my hot dog bun.

Page 75

Students' answers may vary. Sample answers are provided below.

Words with *-un*

sun bun
fun run

Words with *-og*

dog hog
smog fog

Words About Dogs

barking running
sleeping furry

1. jog
2. sun
3. logs
4. fun

Page 78

Students should correctly read the poem by pausing in the indicated places.

Page 79

Students' answers may vary. Sample answers are provided below.

Words with *-ow*

glow blow
show slow

Words with *-ake*

cake rake
shake make

Words About Birthdays

candles party
presents celebrate

1. brakes
2. slowly
3. snakes
4. glow

Page 82

Poem Word	1	2	3	4	5	6
dill						
sweet						
or						
tongue						
pickles						
my						

1. pickes
2. or
3. Answers will vary.

Page 83

Students' answers may vary. Sample answers are provided below.

Words with *-un*

fun bun
spun run

Words with *-ick*

pickle tickle
sick stick

Words About Pickles

dill sweet
green

1. hungry
2. funny
3. sick
4. bunny

Page 86

Begins like *shoes*—shirt, shell, sheep, ship

Ends like *brush*—leash, wash, dish, crash

Page 87

Students' answers may vary. Sample answers are provided below.

Words with *-ain*

rain again
main pain
rainbow

Words with *-een*

green seen
queen teen

Words About Rainbows

beautiful sky
colorful rain

1. seen
2. chained
3. green
4. rainy

Page 90

Page 91

Students' answers may vary. Sample answers are provided below.

Words with *-and*

grand sand
band land

Words with *-ay*

today spray
lay away

Words About Sand Castles

sand buckets
towers waves

1. stay
2. band
3. clay
4. candy

Page 94

1. blood
2. sky
3. snow
4. celery
5. crow
6. canary

Page 95

Students' answers may vary. Sample answers are provided below.

Words with *-een*

green seen
keen spleen

Words with *-ail*

sail rail
snail frail

Words About Sailboats

water sails
boat wind

1. seen
2. tail
3. mailed
4. green

Page 98

One and one are two.

Two and two are four.

Four and four are eight.

Page 99

Students' answers may vary. Sample answers are provided below.

Words with *-ore*

more sore
shore tore

Words with *-and*

and sand
stand land

Words About Math

addition subtraction
numbers problems

1. sand
2. tore
3. band
4. shore

Page 102

Students should have glued the puppet, the teddy bear, and the toy car inside the tox box.

Page 103

Students' answers may vary. Sample answers are provided below.

Words with *-ew*

new chew
flew dew

Words with *-oy*

toy boy
enjoy joy

Words About Toys

fun special
mine toy box

1. toy
2. flew
3. enjoy
4. chew

Page 106

1. ends like *me*
2. does not end like *me*
3. ends like *me*
4. ends like *me*
5. does not end like *me*
6. ends like *me*
7. does not end like *me*
8. ends like *me*
9. does not end like *me*

Page 107

Students' answers may vary. Sample answers are provided below.

Words with *-ee*

tree see

fee flee

Words with *-ing*

hiding going

running king

Words About Hiding

peeking seeking

secret quiet

1. hiding
2. three
3. trees
4. going

Page 110

Check students' maps to ensure that they colored according to the key. Students should have mentioned their home country.

Page 111

Students' answers' may vary. Sample answers are provided below.

Words with *-ane*

plane lane

cane vane

Words with *-y*

fly cry

by my

Words About Flying

sky plane

clouds airport

1. cane
2. sky
3. My
4. crane

Page 114

Rhyming long *i* pairs—fight/sight, mice/rice, right/bite, might/night, fine/pine, kite/light, vine/line

Page 115

Students' answers may vary. Sample answers are provided below.

Words with *-ight*

fight right

light tight

Words with *-im*

him Jimmy

dim slim

Words About Bullies

tough scary

mean

1. fight
2. rim
3. tight
4. trims

Page 118

1. pan + cake = pancake
2. rain + bow = rainbow
3. cow + boy = cowboy
4. star + fish = starfish

Page 119

Students' answers may vary. Sample answers are provided below.

Words with *-ast*

breakfast last

blast fast

Words with *-ate*

plate late

date gate

Words About Pancakes

syrup butter

hot stack

1. late
2. fast
3. state
4. cast

Page 122

Rhymes with rug—bug, tug, shrug, dug, hug, jug, mug, plug

1. Names objects—bug, rug, jug, plug, mug
2. Names actions—shrug, tug dug, hug

Page 123

Students' answers may vary. Sample answers are provided below.

Words with *-ug*

bug rug

shrug tug

Words with *-ade*

made shade

spade fade

Words About Bears

furry brown

honey claws

1. snuggle
2. shade
3. made
4. jug

Page 126

1. yes
2. no
3. yes
4. yes
5. no
6. yes
7. no
8. yes
9. yes

Page 127

Students' answers may vary. Sample answers are provided below.

Words with *-air*

chair stair
hair pair

Words with *-all*

small all
tall hall

Words About Chairs

leg seat
table comfortable

1. chair
2. called
3. stairs
4. taller

Page 130

1. played—d
2. jumped—t
3. followed—d
4. mailed—d
5. brushed—t
6. folded—ed
7. crawled—d
8. helped—t

Page 131

Students' answers may vary. Sample answers are provided below.

Words with *-ump*

jump bump
dump lump

Words with *-ay*

play day
gray clay

Words About Playtime

running sliding
recess friends

1. May
2. pumped
3. tray
4. jumped

Page 134

Students' answers may vary. Sample answers are provided below.

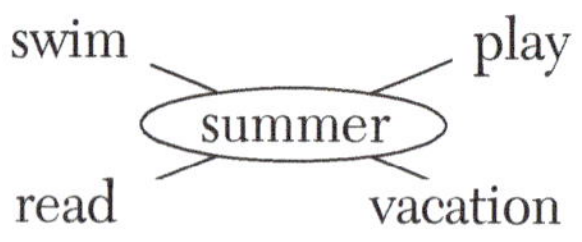

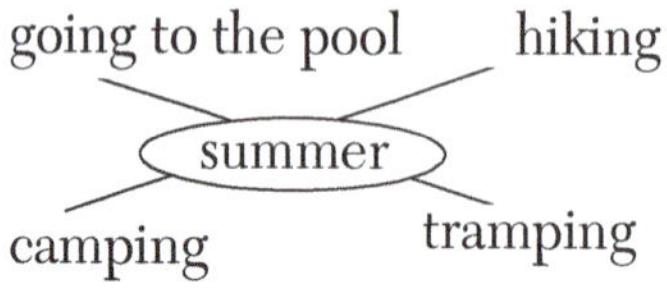

Page 135

Students' answers may vary. Sample answers are provided below.

Words with *-amp*

camping tramping
lamp damp

Words with *-um*

summer bummer
hum tummy

Words About Summer Fun

swimming friends
vacation sun

1. sum
2. camp
3. damp
4. hummed

References Cited

Adams, M. J. 1990. *Beginning to read: Thinking and learning about print.* Cambridge, MA: MIT Press.

Baker, S., D. C. Simmons, and E.J. Kameenui. Eds. 1998. *What reading research tells us about children with diverse learning needs: Bases and basics*. Mahwah, NJ: Erlbaum.

Ball, E. W., and B.A. Blachman. 1991. Does phoneme segmentation training in kindergarten make a difference in early word recognition and developmental spelling? *Reading Research Quarterly* 26:49–86.

Bottomley, D. and J. Osborn. 1993. *Implementing reciprocal teaching with fourth and fifth grade students in content area reading*. ERIC Document 361668.

Bromage, B. K., and R. E. Mayer. 1986. Quantitative and qualitative effects of repetition on learning from technical text. *Journal of Educational Psychology* 78:271–278.

Carter, C. 1997. Why reciprocal teaching? *Educational Leadership* 54:64–68.

Fry, E. 1998. The most common phonograms. *The Reading Teacher* 51:620–622.

Gaskins, I., L. Ehri, C. Cress, C. O'Hara, and K. Donnelly. 1996/1997. Procedures for word learning: Making discoveries about words. *The Reading Teacher* 50:312–328.

Herrell, A., and M. Jordan. 2004. *Fifty strategies for teaching English language learners*. 2nd ed. Upper Saddle, NJ: Pearson Education, Inc.

Hosenfeld, C. 1993. *Activities and materials for implementing adapted versions of reciprocal teaching in beginning, intermediate, and advanced levels of instruction in English, Spanish, and French as a second/foreign language*. ERIC document ED370354.

Jensen, E. 1998. *Teaching with the brain in mind*. Alexandria, VA: Association for Supervision and Curriculum Development.

LaBerge, D., and S. J. Samuels. 1974. Toward a theory of automatic information processing in reading. *Cognitive Psychology* 5:293–323.

National Reading Panel. 2000. *Teaching children to read: An evidence-based assessment of the scientific research literature on reading and its implications for reading instruction.* Report of the National Reading Panel. Washington, DC: U.S. Government Print Office.

O'Shea, L. J., and P. T. Sindelar. 1983. The effects of segmenting written discourse on reading comprehension of low-and high-performance readers. *Reading Research Quarterly* 18:458–465.

Pressley, M. 2002. *Comprehension instruction: What makes sense now, what might make sense soon*. ERIC Document EJ667632.

Rasinski, T. V. 2003. *The Fluent Reader*. New York: Scholastic Professional Books.

Rosenshine, B. and C. Meister. 1994. Reciprocal teaching: A review of the research. *Review of Educational Research* 64:479–530.

Samuels, S. J. 1979. The method of repeated reading. *The Reading Teacher* 32:403–408.

Stanovich, K. E. 1986. Matthew effects in reading: Some consequences of individual differences in the acquisition of literacy. *Reading Research Quarterly* 21:360–407.

WIDA—housed within the Wisconsin Center for Education Research. 2007. English language proficiency standards. The Board of Regents of the University of Wisconsin System, http://www.wida.us/standards/elp.aspx

Yopp, H. K. 1988. The validity and reliability of phonemic awareness tests. *Reading Research Quarterly* 23:159–177.

Yopp, H. K. 1992. Developing phonemic awareness in young children. *The Reading Teacher* 45:696–704.

Contents of the Digital Resources

Accessing the Digital Resources

Digital Resources can be downloaded by following these steps:

1. Go to **www.tcmpub.com/digital**
2. Use the ISBN number to redeem the Digital Resources.

ISBN-13: 978-1-4258-0676-7 — ISBN
90000
9 781425 806767

3. Respond to the question using the book.
4. Follow the prompts on the Content Cloud website to sign in or create a new account.
5. The redeemed content will now be on your My Content screen. Click on the product to look through the Digital Resources. All files can be downloaded, while some files can also be previewed, opened, and shared.

Poems and Activity Pages	
Filenames	
lesson1.pdf	lesson16.pdf
lesson2.pdf	lesson17.pdf
lesson3.pdf	lesson18.pdf
lesson4.pdf	lesson19.pdf
lesson5.pdf	lesson20.pdf
lesson6.pdf	lesson21.pdf
lesson7.pdf	lesson22.pdf
lesson8.pdf	lesson23.pdf
lesson9.pdf	lesson24.pdf
lesson10.pdf	lesson25.pdf
lesson11.pdf	lesson26.pdf
lesson12.pdf	lesson27.pdf
lesson13.pdf	lesson28.pdf
lesson14.pdf	lesson29.pdf
lesson15.pdf	lesson30.pdf

MP3	
(01) Summer's Over	(16) Birthday
(02) I'm Ready	(17) Pickles
(03) The Sun's Glow	(18) The Rainbow
(04) Roller Coaster	(19) Castle
(05) Frozen Treats	(20) Sailboats
(06) The Night-light	(21) Addition
(07) Call Their Name	(22) The Toy Box
(08) A Simple Notion	(23) Peek-a-boo
(09) Video Game	(24) I'll Fly a Plane
(10) Tasty Treats	(25) The Bully
(11) Short or Tall?	(26) Pancakes
(12) Mouse in the House	(27) Snug in a Rug
(13) Oh, Fall!	(28) The Chair
(14) Blueberry Pancakes	(29) Jump for Joy
(15) Babysitting Dogs	(30) Oh, Summer!

Additional Resources	
Item	**Filename**
Instructional Plan	instructional.pdf
McREL Chart	mcrelchart.pdf
Activity Skill Corr. Chart	activitychart.pdf